Don't Chase the Monkey

Stop Reacting, Start Leading: A Guide to Effective Management

Kate Woodward Young, M.Ed.

Carrie Casey

Deneise Eyl Rogers, Editor

Don't Chase the Monkey

ISBN: 978-1-954885-34-9

Dedication

We dedicate this book to the more than four thousand early childcare directors, owners, and heads of school who have continued to inspire us now and over the past twenty-three years.

Table of Contents

Chapter 1

The Adventure Begins

Being a leader is like stepping onto the pages of a "choose your own adventure" book. Every decision you make, every path you take, leads you down a different road. Some roads are smooth and well-lit, while others are tangled, dark, and full of hidden pitfalls.

The choices you make each day determine the kind of leader—and person—you will become. Beware, not all choices are created equal. Some choices can lead to a life of order, satisfaction, and success, while others may plunge you into chaos, stress, and regret.

As you read on, imagine yourself standing at a crossroads. You can only pick one path to embark upon fully knowing that your choice will shape the rest of your journey.

The Curious Climb

You wake up to the shrill sound of your alarm, a wave of dread washing over you as you think through the day ahead. You reach for your phone, only to see one missed call from the regional leader, Susan, and three texts from your opener, Tommy. It's going to be one of those days.

Who should you respond to first, the regional leader or your opener? You decide Tommy gets the first response as the higher priority, because someone must get the place open. You read Tommy's texts and see that his car broke down and he can't cover the cost of an Uber. Great. He can work if you can figure out how to get him there within the next 30 minutes...and he lives 20 minutes from you.

What should you do? You consider several options: go open yourself, call around to find him a ride, or pay for a Lyft out of your pocket? Paying for the Lyft seems like the easiest solution.

Okay, good start to the day, one problem down. Now, onto the voicemail from Susan. You listen to Susan's voicemail and brace yourself for what's next. Her voice is calm, almost too calm, like the calm before the storm that you know is about to hit. "Hey, just wanted to give you a heads-up," she begins. "Corporate's pushing through a new initiative—something about streamlining our customer feedback process. I know it's the last minute, but we need to have everything prepped and ready to roll out by the end of the day. That's a 5 p.m. deadline. I'll send over the details in an email, but you'll need to brief the team, adjust the workflow, and ensure the new system is in place for tomorrow's opening."

You sigh, rubbing your temples as you try to process the task ahead. A 12-hour turnaround for a new project is tight, especially with everything else you've got on your plate. But this isn't optional. Susan's tone made that clear—it's one of those "make it happen" situations.

As you mentally prepare for the day ahead, you glance at the clock. It's time to get the kids up. You head down the hallway to their rooms, hoping that the morning routine will go smoothly, but know, deep down, that's probably wishful thinking.

You start with your youngest, who's usually the easiest to wake up. "Good morning, sunshine," you say softly, pulling back the curtains to let in the morning light. They stir a bit but stay buried under the covers. You lean down and gently nudge them.

"Time to get up, sweetheart. We've got a big day ahead."

A sleepy mumble escapes from beneath the blanket, something along the lines of "Five more minutes..." You smile to yourself: classic.

Next, you move on to your oldest. This one's always a bit more of a challenge. As you open the door, you're met with a groan. "Come on, we've got to get moving," you say, as you try to keep your voice upbeat.

"Nooo, I'm not going to school today," they grumble, pulling the blanket over their head. You sigh, internally, knowing you've got a battle on your hands.

"Why not?" you ask, leaning against the doorframe.

"I just don't want to," comes the muffled reply. "Can't I just stay home? I'm tired, and I have nothing important to do today anyway."

You check the time again, knowing that each minute counts this morning. But you also know that forcing the issue will only make things worse. You take a deep breath, deciding how best to approach this. Do you lay down the law, coax them out of bed with promises of a fun after-school activity, or let them have a few more minutes and risk running late? ...all while that 5 p.m. deadline looms over your head.

You lean down, pulling the blanket back just enough to see their sleepy face. "I get it, you're tired," you say, trying to keep your tone understanding but firm. "But we've got to keep going, just like I must get to work. Tell you what, if we can make it through today, maybe we can do something special this weekend. How does that sound?"

There's a pause and then finally, a reluctant nod. It's not a victory, but it's a step in the right direction. You pat their shoulder and head back to the youngest, who's now halfway out of bed, rubbing their eyes.

As you guide them through getting dressed, brushing teeth, and packing bags, your mind is already juggling the day's tasks—Tommy's delayed start, Susan's project, as well as the usual fires you'll have to put out once you step foot in the office. But, for now, it's all about getting the kids ready and out the door. One step at a time, you remind yourself, one step at a time.

You finally take a deep breath and listen to Susan's voicemail again. She needs you to pull together a detailed report on the team's productivity for the last quarter. Not only does she want it in her inbox by the end of the day, but she also expects you to present it during a virtual meeting at 4 PM. Your clock is ticking, and it's only 7:15 AM.

With additional weight now added to your shoulders, you head upstairs to check on the kids' progress toward "up and ready for their day." As soon as you open the door, you're greeted by a muffled groan. Your oldest, Jake, is buried under the covers, clearly not thrilled about leaving the comfort of his bed. You try to coax him out with promises of pancakes this weekend, but it's a losing battle.

After what feels like an eternity, Jake finally drags himself out of bed. Then another problem hits: you realize you're out of the usual snacks—no granola bars, no fruit snacks, nothing that'll pass without a fuss. You grab a couple of apples from the fridge and hope for the best.

But of course, the best isn't enough. Jake takes one look at the apple in his lunchbox and his face crumples. He starts crying, stomping his foot. "I don't want this! I want my granola bar!" His little sister, Emma, takes her cue from older brother and starts whining too, and she hasn't even looked in her bag yet.

The clock is ticking and every minute feels like an hour. You try reasoning, bribing, and even threatening, to no avail. The tantrum continues. Finally, you manage to calm Jake down by promising to pick up the granola bars after school, though you know the odds of that happening are slim given today's lineup.

With the kids reluctantly settled, you rush to the bedroom to wake up your spouse. As usual, he seems blissfully oblivious to the chaos downstairs. You give him a gentle shake, reminding him that his meeting starts in 45 minutes. He mumbles something unintelligible and pulls the blanket over his head, but at least he's awake.

You glance at the clock—8:10 AM. You should have left the house five minutes ago! Panic starts to set in as you frantically gather your things, usher the kids out the door, and try to keep your stress from spilling over. The kids drag their feet, the front door sticks, and you can feel the seconds slipping away. After all the lollygagging, finally, you're in the car. This day already feels like a train wreck, and it's barely begun.

You hustle the kids into the car, doing a quick headcount to make sure no one's left behind. Jake sulks in the backseat while Emma clutches her apple like it's the last thing she'll ever eat. You hurriedly throw your bag into the passenger seat, buckle up, and start the engine.

Just as you're about to pull out of the driveway, you notice the gas gauge hovering precariously close to empty. Excellent—that's just what you need. You make a mental note to stop for gas after work. You know you will be cutting it close with everything else on your plate. Oh, well, there's no time to dwell on it now.

You drive through the morning traffic, trying to keep the kids entertained while you navigate the usual bottlenecks. The radio plays something upbeat, but you can barely enjoy it with everything rapidly replaying through your mind: Tommy's late start, Susan's last-minute project, your husband still defiantly in the bed and now the looming low fuel issue.

Finally, you reach the school. The kids start to unbuckle as soon as you pull into the drop-off lane. You help them gather their backpacks, give each one a quick kiss on the head, and send them on their way with a forced smile and a reminder to be good.

Just as you're about to pull away, a PTA mom taps on your window. Why must she smile so brightly this early in the morning? You roll down the window, and she hands you a colorful flier. "Don't forget about the PTA fundraiser next week!" she chirps. "We're counting on you, Chairperson Extraordinaire!"

You think to yourself, "WHAT?! Chairperson Extraordinaire?!" Your stomach drops as the title hits you like a ton of bricks. You completely forgot that you'd agreed to chair the fundraiser for Emma's grade. Now, on top of everything else, you must organize an event, rally other parents, and somehow not lose your mind in the process.

You plaster on a smile, thank her, and shove the flier into the glove compartment—one more thing to add to your never-ending to-do list. As you drive away, you can't help but wonder if you've bitten off more than you can chew this time. The days barely started, and it feels like you're already running on empty—literally and figuratively.

As you drive away from the school, you glance at the clock and realize you're making decent time—maybe you can even grab those supplies you need for work before things get too crazy. You quickly decide to swing by the store. It's a quick stop, just a few items, but as you rush through the aisles, you realize your stomach growls loudly. With everything that's happened this morning, you haven't had a chance to eat anything. You toss a few more items into your basket, calculating how long a quick detour through a drive-through will take.

You're back in the car within minutes, juggling bags of supplies on the passenger seat. The drive-through line is mercifully short, and soon, you're pulling away with a breakfast sandwich and a much-needed large coffee. The first sip hits your system like a lifeline. You take another quick bite of the sandwich as you drive, trying to savor what little calm you can manage before the workday really begins.

But, as you turn the corner and your workplace comes into view, your hard-earned bit of calm shatters. You spot a small crowd of angry-looking customers milling around the front door, glancing at their watches and muttering to each other. You feel your heart sink when you realize what's happened: Tommy isn't here yet.

You park quickly, shove your half-eaten sandwich back into the bag, and rush to the door. The customers spot you and immediately start voicing their frustrations—some have been waiting for over fifteen minutes. You fumble with the keys, apologizing as you unlock the doors and usher them inside. "Sorry for the delay," you say with a forced smile, trying to smooth things over. "We had some unforeseen circumstances this morning," you say loudly.

As the customers stream in, you glance around the empty store, and the weight of the day's chaos begins to settle on your shoulders. There's no one else here to help you set up, no one to take over while you catch your breath. You're going to have to manage the opening all on your own.

You hang up your coat, shove the breakfast sandwich into a drawer, and take a deep breath. The door is open, the customers are inside, and the day is just getting started. You've been putting out fires since you woke up, and it looks like that won't change anytime soon. But somehow, you'll get through it—because that's what you do. You're the leader; this is just another day in life. Putting out fires has become your way of life.

As you're trying to manage the influx of customers, you finally see Tommy and another staff person rushing through the door, looking flustered and apologetic. "Sorry, sorry, sorry," Tommy mumbles, not quite meeting your eyes as he hurries to his station. The other staff member gives you a quick nod before diving into their work.

Relief washes over you as they start to oversee the client responsibilities. The customers seem to calm down now that they're being attended to, and the tension in the room eases slightly. You catch Tommy's eye and offer a quick smile, hoping to convey that everything's okay—for now, at least. With the front of the house taken care of, you head to the office, feeling the weight of the morning's chaos lifting just a little.

Once inside the office, you close the door behind you and let out a long breath. Finally, a moment to catch up and get organized. You sit down at your desk and check the voicemail first. You unconsciously brace yourself for whatever might be waiting.

Susan, the regional leader, left another message. As her voice fills the room, calm but insistent, she rattles off a list of things she needs by the end of the day and explains more details on the project she mentioned earlier. She also leaves you with updates on a few other ongoing issues.

You jot down the tasks as you listen, trying to keep them in order. Next, you open your email. Your heart sinks into your stomach as you see the number of unread messages. It's even worse than you feared. Requests, questions, reminders, all piled up in your inbox.

The urgency of some is unmistakable, while others are marked "ASAP" or "IMPORTANT" in bold letters. Now, you feel like you could just cry. Maybe staying in bed like your husband definitely feels like a good choice.

You feel an all too familiar sense of overwhelm creeping in. You dutifully push it aside. It's time to triage. You quickly scan through the emails, sorting them into categories: urgent, can wait, and delegate. As you work through them, you start forming a mental map of your day—what needs to be tackled first, what can be pushed to later, and what can be handed off to someone else.

The clock ticks instantly and you know there's no time to lose. You've survived the first hour, but the day is far from over. With your list in hand, you're ready to dive into the next round of challenges. Because no matter what comes your way, you're going to keep going—just like you always do.

With your to-do list set, you leave the office to begin your morning walkthrough. As you move through the building, you make mental notes of everything that needs attention—a loose door handle here, some clutter that needs tidying up there. The familiar routine comforts you for a moment, as it allows you to see everything with fresh eyes. Practice ensures that the day will run smoothly.

Just as you're finishing up, one of your staff members catches your attention. "Hey, can I talk to you for a sec?" they ask, looking a little sheepish. You nod, already sensing what's coming.

"I was wondering if I could take Friday off," they continued, explaining the reason for the request. You quickly run through the schedule in your head, assessing whether you can afford to be one person short at the end of the week. After a moment, you nod. "We can make it work," you say, making a note to adjust the schedule later.

No sooner have you handled that request when another staff member approaches. "Can you cover my station for a few minutes? I need to use the restroom," they ask. You agree, stepping in to keep things moving while they take a quick break. It's a small task, but it feels like one more thing added to the growing list of demands on your time.

Just as you head back to your office, a third staff member approaches, looking slightly frazzled. "We're out of paper towels, can you grab me some?" they ask you, then proceed to list off other items they need. You mentally add another task to your morning, knowing that without those supplies, she won't be successful. "I'll grab them for you," you say, heading to the storage area and quickly restocking what's needed.

With those immediate requests handled, you finally make your way back to the office. You feel like you've already put in a full days work, and you haven't started on the tasks from the regional leader. There's no time to dwell on it. You've got a deadline to meet, and the clock ticks.

You sit down at your desk, take a deep breath, and focus on the work ahead. It's been a whirlwind of a morning, but now it's time to buckle down and get the project done. You know there will be more interruptions, translating to more demands on your already stretched time and energy. For now, you've carved out a little space to concentrate—and you're determined to make the most of it.

You're the leader, which seems to mean you're just managing to hold it all together. It feels like you're a traveler lost in a labyrinth, where every turn reveals a new obstacle. Your to-do list is overwhelming, a tangled web of tasks that seem to multiply by the minute.

By the time you finally head home, your mind races. You replay the day's events, thinking of all the things that went wrong, all the things you should have done differently. Sleep doesn't come quickly; when it is, it's filled with restless dreams of unfinished tasks and unsolved problems.

That's the path you chose. Now, let's look at the other possible path:

The Path Less Traveled

The sun rises. You wake up with a sense of purpose and anticipation. Today is another day in your journey as a leader, and you're ready for the adventure ahead. You know challenges will come, but you've equipped yourself with the tools and strategies to handle them.

You've trained yourself to face the day with a clear plan and a structured approach. You reach for your phone and see one missed call from the regional leader, Susan, and three texts from your opener, Tommy. You take a breath, knowing you've got the tools to handle whatever comes your way.

You decide to prioritize Tommy since getting the place open is essential. Instead of solving the problem for him, you text back, "Tommy, please call or text other team members to find someone to cover the opening shift. Then, take your time to figure out how to get in today. Let me know if you haven't found a solution by 10, and we'll problem-solve together. Get to work as soon as you can."

You then return Susan's call. You tell her you will start working on the new project after completing the morning routine. You set a clear time when you'll check in with an update on your progress, managing her expectations upfront.

You move on to check on the kids, but you're greeted with children getting themselves moving - part of the new system you implemented to ensure they start taking responsibility for their morning routine. Lunch was packed the night before, so there's no need to rush through the kitchen in a frenzy.

However, when you hand over the backpacks, you realize you're out of their favorite snacks. You offer a substitution, and one child starts to protest.

Instead of letting the situation escalate, you calmly remind them that they chose the snack the night before and explain that today, they'll need to make do with what's available. "Remember, you helped pack these snacks last night. Tomorrow, we can make a different choice, okay?"

With the kids settled you head to wake up your spouse. You remind them of the time and leave the room, confident they'll manage their morning routine.

You're ready to leave, but you notice the car is low on gas. Instead of letting this become an immediate problem, you make a note to fill up after work. This can be handled when you add it to the plan.

You drop the kids off and receive a flier for the PTA fundraiser you agreed to chair. Instead of adding this to today's list of things to do, you set it aside for later review when you can give it the attention it deserves.

Since the morning went well, you have plenty of time to stop for supplies. You also grab a quick bite at the drive-through, ensuring you're fueled for the day. As you pull into the parking lot, you smile to see Janice's car in the lot, along with several customer cars.

You calmly walk in and greet Janice with a smile. You visited with a couple of customers you know and thank Janice for coming in early.

You head to your office, but instead of diving into every voicemail and email, you stick to your plan. You triage the messages, sorting out the ones that need immediate attention and delegating tasks where appropriate. The ones that can wait are scheduled for later, ensuring your focus remains on what's most critical.

During your walkthrough, you encounter staff with various requests. Instead of taking on these tasks yourself, you guide them to the appropriate solutions:

- You direct the staff member who needs a day off later in the week to the proper channel. She will complete a day-off request form and follow the standard approval process.
- You state that you appreciate the heads-up and remind them that you'll review it during the next scheduled check-in.
- You suggest the staff member who needs a short break to radio the floater to cover for them. You reinforce the importance of effectively utilizing the team.
- You show the third staff member who needs supplies where the extra keys are kept. You give them express permission to access supplies when needed, empowering them to handle them independently next time.

With the immediate tasks and walkthrough complete, you head back to your office to start on the project from Susan. You've managed to handle the morning's challenges without taking on unnecessary monkeys, and now you can focus on the work that requires your attention.

As the day progresses, you encounter challenges without overwhelming you. You've learned to manage your time effectively, focusing on the tasks that truly matter. You confidently delegate, knowing your team is capable and ready to take on responsibilities. The load shared feels lighter because everyone contributes.

You've built a culture of accountability and growth. When problems arise, your team doesn't shy away from them. Instead, they come to you with solutions, eager to take leadership and learn from their experiences. You're not the only one solving problems—everyone is involved, and together, you're stronger.

By the end of the day, you feel a sense of accomplishment. The tasks on your to-do list have been handled efficiently, and you created a clear plan for tomorrow. You leave work with energy to spare, excited to spend time with your loved ones, pursue hobbies, or relax. You sleep soundly, knowing you're in control of your journey, not just surviving it.

The weeks and months pass, and you see the fruits of your efforts. Your team is thriving, your projects are on track, and you're growing as a leader. The path you've chosen challenges and rewards you. The adventure you're on is one of discovery, learning, and mastery. You've learned to navigate twists and turns, overcome obstacles, and lead confidently.

You tamed the chaos and turned it into order. You're living the life of a successful leader. The to-do items are managed, prioritized, and completed with precision. You're free to explore new horizons, take on new challenges, and continue your journey of growth and success.

A Glimpse of What Lies Ahead

But wait. What about the first path? The one where chaos reigns, the to-do items are everywhere, and the labyrinth threatens to trap you forever? What are these to-do items, and how did they get there? More importantly, how can you avoid them and ensure that your adventure stays on the path of mastery?

The choice is yours. But first, you need to understand those to-do items and how to keep them from piling up and overwhelming you. Turn the page to discover the secrets of successful management and learn how to choose your adventure wisely. The journey has only just begun.

Chapter 2

The Daily "Monkeys" of a Leader

In a leader's life, the "monkeys on their back" are the tasks and responsibilities that follow them day in and day out. These include routine tasks, responding to emails, conducting team meetings, reviewing performance metrics, managing team conflicts, and planning future projects. While each task is manageable on its own, together they accumulate and may create a sense of constant pressure.

In the last chapter, you read about a lot of different monkeys:

- Reports
- Covering shifts
- Packing lunch
- Waking children
- Getting gas
- Covering for staff
- Getting supplies
- Replying to emails
- What did I miss?

For most leaders, the daily flood of emails is a persistent chattering "monkey" that requires constant attention. Responding to team members, clients, and upper management can take up a significant portion of the day. Ignoring this "monkey" can lead to miscommunication, missed opportunities, and escalating issues that become harder to manage over time.

Regular team meetings are essential for keeping everyone aligned and informed. However, these meetings also represent a recurring task that requires preparation, follow-up and managing differing opinions or conflicts. The "monkey" here is the ongoing need to facilitate productive conversations, ensure that everyone's voice is heard, and steer the team toward the company's goals.

Providing feedback and conducting performance reviews is another responsibility that weighs on leaders. This "monkey" involves not just the act of giving feedback but also the emotional labor of doing so in a constructive, encouraging manner. It's a task that requires sensitivity, clarity, and a deep understanding of each team member's strengths and areas for improvement.

Ensuring that projects stay on track and deadlines are met is a daily "monkey" for leaders. This task involves constant monitoring, adjusting plans, and often, dealing with unforeseen challenges. The pressure of meeting deadlines and delivering results can feel like a monkey that is always there, reminding the leader of their responsibility to keep everything moving forward.

Managing interpersonal conflicts within a team is a delicate and ongoing challenge. The "monkey" in this scenario is the need to address issues promptly and fairly, maintaining team harmony while also being decisive. Conflict resolution requires a balance of empathy and authority. The stress of managing these situations can feel like a heavy burden on a leader's back.

Beyond daily tasks, leaders are also responsible for looking ahead and setting the strategic direction for their teams. This involves planning for future projects, identifying growth opportunities, and ensuring the team's work aligns with broader organizational goals.

The "monkey" here is the ongoing responsibility to innovate, adapt, and stay ahead of the curve, all while managing the day-to-day operations.

Given the weight of these daily "monkeys," leaders need effective strategies to manage their tasks and maintain balance. Here are some approaches that can help:

Not all tasks are created equally. Effective prioritization is key to managing the daily monkeys. Choosing which tasks are critical, which to delegate and which to delay allows leaders to focus their energy on what truly matters. One of the most powerful and efficient tools available to a leader is delegation. Properly training and trusting team members with responsibilities grants leaders a lighter load and empowers others to grow in their roles. This helps leaders manage the daily monkeys and fosters a collaboratively motivated team.

Effective time management techniques, such as time blocking, can help leaders stay on top of their tasks. Allocating specific time periods for emails, meetings, and focused work; leaders can ensure that no single "monkey" monopolizes their attention.

Taking time to reflect on what's working and what's not is crucial for long-term success. Leaders who regularly assess their workload and adjust their strategies equip themselves to handle the daily challenges coming their way.

Leaders shouldn't carry all the monkeys alone. Building a strong support network of peers, mentors, and team members provides valuable insights, advice, and assistance. This network can help leaders navigate their responsibilities more effectively and reduce the feeling of being overwhelmed.

While the metaphor of "monkeys on your back" describes the daily burdens leaders face, we must recognize the racial sensitivities associated with the term "monkey." Historically, racist caricatures dehumanized people of African descent by comparing them to monkeys. These harmful depictions have been used to discriminate and justify violence. They continue to impact society today.

Given this context, it's essential to use the phrase "monkey on your back" with an awareness of its potential implications. In professional and public settings, it may be advisable to consider alternative metaphors that avoid the risk of perpetuating racial stereotypes. Phrases like "carrying a burden" or "bearing a weight" can convey similar meanings without invoking harmful imagery.

Chapter 3

Who's Got the Monkey

"Who's Got the Monkey?" is a management concept popularized by William Oncken Jr. and Donald L. Wass in their 1974 Harvard Business Review (HBR) article titled "Management Time: Who's Got the Monkey?" This concept uses the monkey metaphor to describe tasks. The burden of responsibility metaphorically shifts tasks as the monkey climbs to and from leaders and subordinates. Leaders often take on too many monkeys that could be delegated to their team members. Leaders with too many monkeys on their backs leads to inefficiency and burnout.

The concept of "Who's Got the Monkey?" has been widely adopted by organizations prioritizing effective delegation and time management. Some companies known to incorporate this management concept include:

1. General Electric (GE) - GE is well known for its rigorous management training programs. The "Who's Got the Monkey?" concept aligns well with GE's focus on delegation and empowering leaders to lead more effectively by ensuring that responsibilities are appropriately assigned.

2. IBM - As a technology and consulting giant, IBM strongly emphasizes management training and leadership development. The "Who's Got the Monkey?" concept has been used in various contexts within IBM to help leaders better delegate tasks and responsibilities.

3. Procter & Gamble (P&G): P&G is known for its robust leadership development programs. The "Who's Got the Monkey?" concept fits into their management philosophy of empowering employees and ensuring leaders focus on strategic rather than tactical work.

4. Google: Known for its innovative management practices, Google has adopted various management concepts, including "Who's Got the Monkey?" to encourage effective delegation and to ensure that leaders are not overwhelmed with tasks that their teams can manage.

5. Harvard Business School (HBS): While not a company, HBS is the publisher of the original article and frequently includes "Who's Got the Monkey?" in its teaching management and leadership curriculum.

6. Microsoft: Microsoft's management training often incorporates delegation and time management lessons, where "Who's Got the Monkey?" is highly relevant. This concept helps Microsoft leaders focus on high-priority strategic tasks by delegating operational responsibilities to their teams.

7. Coca-Cola: Coca-Cola has emphasized leadership development and effective management strategies, including the delegation principles outlined in "Who's Got the Monkey?" This helps their leaders lead more efficiently and maintain focus on the company's broader goals.

These companies and many others have embraced the "Who's Got the Monkey?" concept in their broader management practices. The idea remains relevant because it addresses a common challenge in management: leaders' tendency to take on tasks that should be delegated, which can hinder their own effectiveness and the growth of their team members.

Chapter 4

Our Version of Original Article

There is a Polish saying, "Not my circus. Not my monkeys." That saying is one of my favorites. I am constantly saying, *"Not my monkey"* now. I used to be a monkey-chaser.

- Carrie and I both fought as young entrepreneurs to be liked by clients and staff. We wanted to be taken seriously and have staff, and clients understand that we knew what we were doing. We thought we needed to be more focused on customer service and that this would be a great benefit to our clients and secure client retention. Although we had different businesses in different states, we both struggled with balancing our to-do lists.

- Because I wanted to control my work hours and connect with clients at their locations, I would let them control what time and how long our appointments lasted. Rarely did an appointment last the scheduled amount of time, and even more often, I would give away advice that had nothing to do with the service provided.

- For example, clients would hire my company to do printing and layout work. However, I often discussed finance, sales, and marketing during client appointments. One client even asked for advice on hiring. I quickly realized that I needed to be in control of my time or the energy I was pouring into my clients.

When Carrie first opened her business, she wanted to ensure everyone knew she was a caring and empathetic boss. She wanted her employees to know that she cared about them and wanted them at her business, that she would take good care of them.

She had an employee who was probably about twice as old as she was. The employee had multiple children, the youngest of which was a teenager. One day, the employee came into work and was just a mess, an emotional wreck. Carrie asked her what was going on. The employee responded that she had the worst morning ever and told her a long, involved story about all kinds of teenage behavior.

The teenage son was being a twit and saying extremely rude things to his mother. Carrie was concerned that this was borderline abuse. She just kept listening.

After the employee purged herself of all the morning horrors, Carrie got her back to the point where she could work. Carrie spent the rest of the morning looking for resources on how the staff member could help this teenager. The staff person already had three adult children, had managed teenagers before, and knew how to do it, but Carrie thought as her boss, it was her job to go out and find additional resources.

Carrie's eldest was only three. She didn't have personal experience to draw from; Carrie had to seek everything out. Carrie didn't want another day when her employee was a complete wreck and couldn't work the first part of her shift.

So, she chose to chase the monkey.

After helping her purge the poison, Carrie should have asked, "Do you need any help from me?" If she said yes, then ask what help she needs. Only then should Carrie have gone and gotten the resources.

Often, people need to vent.

One way to keep conversations to a reasonable time and on one topic in advance is to set an expectation up front by giving a timeframe: *"I have fifteen minutes before I need to give Matthew a break. Do you want to talk?"* That is the right way to manage a monkey like this.

As I said, I did a lot early on in my leadership career. I wanted to be the good guy, so I chased down every monkey and treated them as my own. I was robbing others of the ability to fight their own battles and myself of the ability to get my work done. I did it with others' personal problems and their work. It was unintentionally disrespectful. I didn't respect their ability to handle challenges.

For example, I would go out and get supplies that were mentioned but should have been written on the supply list. If I learned that they desperately needed this, that, or whatever, I would drop what I was doing and go get it for them. I took care of all their monkeys.

Now, I have learned to manage my time more effectively. One way I do so is by recognizing who a monkey belongs to. I constantly say, *"Not my monkey."* I want you to learn about this superpower, too.

Did you know the average leader makes it in less than a year? Most new businesses close in the first year. That is a ridiculous burnout rate, and the number one reason is constantly taking care of someone else's monkeys instead of bringing in revenue.

Learn to recognize those monkeys. Learn to determine if it is your monkey. Learn to manage them. Learn that you absolutely cannot take care of other people's monkeys.

So, say it with me, right now, out loud: *"Not my circus, not my monkeys!"*

I immediately connected when I first read the article "Management

Time: Who's Got the Monkey?" by William Oncken and Donald Wass in the Harvard Business Review. I have absorbed its lessons and used them throughout my life since. I use these principles in my work and business life but also raising teenagers. We wrote this book because we have seen the impact of teaching a few thousand leaders and Early Childcare Directors for years as the Monkey Ladies. These are some of our most popular training sessions. Let's explore how the concept of Monkey Management applies to your business and your personal life.

In any business, the leader has demands coming at her from many directions: business partners, leaders, peers, customers, and staff, to name a few. These demands limit the leader's autonomy. The leader needs to do something for them to get active support for all aspects of their business. The business partner needs a report, the client an account statement, and the team member coverage for a day off. These requests take up so much of the leader's time that successful leadership hinges on her ability to control this "monkey on her back" effectively.

Why is it that the administrative team typically needs more time while their staff is running out of work and looking for a chance to check their phone? What does time management mean as it relates to the interaction between leaders, partners, their leaders, and their staff?

Specifically, leaders have five different kinds of time:

Boss-imposed time – to accomplish the activities the boss/ partner requires, which she cannot disregard without direct and swift penalty. This includes agencies that are the "boss" of you such as regulatory agencies, inspection and taxing entities.

System-imposed time – to accommodate requests from the administrative team that has active support from her peers. This assistance must also be provided unless there are penalties, though not always direct or swift, such as employment files and various inspections of buildings, equipment, or processes.

Client imposed time - to provide quality customer service or quality product/service.

Staff imposed time - to support staff and contractors who work for you and your business.

Self-imposed time – to do things the administrative team originates or agrees to do.

The remaining part of the day will be your own and is called "discretionary time." This is the time to focus on your priorities, like planning, strategizing, evaluating, and revising other's work.

Self-imposed time is not subject to repercussions. The boss/partner nor the system can discipline the leader for not doing what they did not know the partner had intended to do in the first place.

Management of time requires the management team to get control over the timing and content of what they do. Since what their bosses and the system imposed on them can have negative consequences, leaders cannot adjust those requirements. So, their self-imposed time becomes their major area of concern.

Leaders should increase the discretionary component of their self-imposed time by minimizing or doing away with the "staff" component. They will then use the added period to get better control over their boss-imposed and system-imposed activities. Most leaders spend much more staff-imposed time than they even faintly realize. Hence, we shall use the analogy of a monkey on their back to examine how staff-imposed time comes into being and what the leader can do about it.

All these tasks, regardless of who assigned them, are the monkeys we must manage. Let's explore what this looks like in practice.

Where Is the Monkey?

Let us imagine that the leader is walking down the hall and then she notices one of her staff, Marie, coming up the hallway. When they are next to one another, Marie greets the leader with, *"Good morning. We've got a problem. You see..."*

As Marie continues, the leader recognizes this problem. It has the same two characteristics common to many problems her staff gratuitously brings to her attention. Namely, the leader knows (a) enough to get involved, but (b) not enough to make the on-the-spot decision expected of her. Eventually, the leader says, *"So glad you brought this up. I'm in a rush right now. Meanwhile, let me think about it and I'll let you know."* Then she and Marie parted company.

Let us analyze what has just happened. Before the two of them met, on whose back was the monkey. The staff member. Now, whose back is it on? The leader. Staff-imposed time begins when a monkey successfully executes a leap from the back of a staff member to the back of the leader. The staff-imposed directive ends once the monkey is returned to its proper handler for care and feeding.

By taking on the monkey, the leader has willingly placed herself in a position where she is now accountable to her staff. Accepting this responsibility from Marie and committing to providing a progress update, the leader took on the responsibility of this monkey effectively making Marie the leader's supervisor in this situation.

Marie—to ensure the leader does not miss this point—will later stick her head in the office and cheerily query, "How's it coming?" This is called "supervision."

Let us imagine again that, in concluding a working conference with another staff member, Lucy, the leader's parting words are, *"Fine. Send me a message about that."* Let's watch where this monkey goes.

The monkey is now on the staff's back because the next move is her, but it is poised for a leap. *Watch that monkey*. Lucy dutifully writes the requested message and sends it to the leader. Shortly after that, the leader plucks it from her account and reads it. Whose move is it now? The leader. If she does not make the next move soon, she will get a follow-up question from the staff. This is yet another form of misplaced supervision.

The longer the leader delays, the more frustrated the staff will become as the leader is, "spinning her wheels." The leader will feel more and more guilty as her backlog of staff-imposed time continues to mount.

Let's suppose once again that in a meeting with a third staff member, Hallie, the leader, agrees to provide all the necessary backing for a marketing campaign she has just asked Hallie to develop. The leaders parting words to her are, *"Just let me know how I can help."*

Now let us analyze this scenario. Here the monkey is initially on the staff's back, but for how long? *Watch that monkey.*

Hallie realizes that she cannot let the leader "know" until her proposal has the leader's approval. From experience, she also realizes that her proposal will likely be sitting at the boss 'desk for weeks, waiting for her to eventually get to it.

Who really got the monkey? Who will be checking up on whom? Wheel spinning and bottlenecking are on their way again. The leader steadily collects more monkeys.

A fourth staff person, Stephen, has just been transferred from another location to launch and eventually manage a newly created division. The leader quickly meets with Stephen. She plans an obscure future meeting, "soon" to hammer out a set of objectives for the new job. The leader ends the encounter with, *"I will draw up an initial draft for discussion with you."*

Let us analyze this one, too. The staff has a new job, by formal assignment, and the full responsibility by formal delegation. Did you catch that? However, the leader left holding the monkey and still has the next move. Until she makes it, she will have the monkey, and the staff stays immobilized.

Why does it all happen? In each instance, the management team and the staff assume at the outset, wittingly or unwittingly, that the matter under consideration is a joint problem. The monkey, in each case, begins its career astride both their backs. All it must do now is move the wrong leg, and presto! The staff deftly disappears.

The leader acquired yet another acquisition to her menagerie. Of course, monkeys can be trained not to move the wrong leg. It is significantly easier to prevent them from straddling their backs in the first place. Besides, everyone knows that an anxious monkey expresses its frustration by flinging poo on you! No one wants monkey poo.

Who Is Working for Whom?

To make what follows more credible, let us suppose these same four staffers are extremely thoughtful and considerate of the leader's time. Imagine they go to great lengths to allow no more than three monkeys to leap to their boss on any given day. That seems reasonable, wouldn't you agree? It sure seems reasonable! However, simple multiplication shows us the leader will have picked up 60 screaming monkeys in a week! That is far too many monkeys to feed and care for individually. She ends up spending the staff-imposed time juggling her "priorities," which are really all her staff's monkeys. Who is working for whom?

Late Friday afternoon, the leader is in her office with the door closed for privacy, contemplating the situation. Her staff is waiting outside to get a last chance before the weekend to remind her that she must "fish or cut bait."

As they wait, imagine what they are saying to each other about the leader: *"What a bottleneck." "She just can't make up her mind." "How anyone ever got that high up in our industry without being able to make a decision, we'll never know."* Worst of all, the leader cannot make any of these next moves because her time is almost entirely eaten up in meeting her boss-imposed and system-imposed requirements.

To get control of these, she needs discretionary time that she chose to forfeit when she took on everyone else's monkeys. The leader is caught in her self-created vicious cycle.

To make an understatement: time's a-wastin. The leader calls her support team on the messaging app and instructs them to tell her staff that she will be unavailable to see them until Monday morning. She has a lot of monkeys to feed before then.

At 7:00 p.m., she drives home, intending with firm resolve to return to the business tomorrow to catch up over the weekend. She returns bright and early the next day. On her way to the business, she passes the four staff members together playing tennis. That really blows her skirt up! How could they play over the weekend when she has their monkeys to feed?

That does it. She now knows who is really working for whom. She now clearly sees that once she finishes caring for all these monkeys, the staff will surely bring her more. In short, she now sees – with the clarity of a revelation on a mountaintop – that the more she gets caught up, the more she will fall behind. Oh, she sure has some decisions to make this weekend and some changes to implement next week.

She leaves the office faster than a person running away from a plague. Her plan is to get caught up on something else she hasn't had time for in years: a weekend with her friends and family. She essentially denied herself discretionary recreational time in exchange for monkey care for far too long!

She enjoys ten hours of sweet, untroubled slumber Sunday night because she decided upon clear-cut plans for Monday. She is going to get rid of her staff-imposed time. Instead, she will gain an equal amount of discretionary time. Part of that time will be well spent training her staff in the difficult art called "The Care and Feeding of Monkeys."

The leader will also have plenty of discretionary time to control the timing and content of her boss-imposed time and system-imposed time. All of this may take months, but compared with the way things have been, the rewards will be enormous. Her ultimate objective is to manage her management time.

Getting Rid of the Monkeys

The leader starts Monday morning strategically. She arrives just late enough to permit her four staff to gather outside her office. Of course, they want to see her about their monkeys. She calls them in, one by one. She has her questions and directives ready. The purpose of each interview is to take a monkey, place it on the desk between them, and figure out together how to move the monkey to the staff's care.

For some monkeys, this may take some doing. The staff's next move may be so elusive that the monkey sleeps on the staff's back overnight. It is important that the staff members take responsibility to plan the next move. The leader will assign a time to return with it to continue the joint quest for a more substantive move by the staff. The leader intends to squarely place the monkey where it belongs. Using good communication skills, the leader clearly moves the monkey to the proper shoulders. She sets a meeting for the next day to hear the potential solutions. Monkeys sleep just as soundly overnight on the staff's backs as on the leaders.

As each staff member leaves the office, the leader is rewarded by the sight of a monkey leaving her office on the proper back. For the next 24 hours, the staff will not be waiting for the leader. Instead, the leader will be waiting for the staff, and all monkeys will be placed with their rightful caretaker.

Later, as if to remind herself that there is no law against her engaging in a constructive exercise in the interim, the leader strolls down the hallways passing workstations, sticks her head in the door, and cheerily asks, *"How's it coming?"* The time consumed in doing this is discretionary for the leader and boss-imposed for the staff.

When the staff with the monkey on her back and the leader meet at the appointed hour the next day, the leader explains the ground rules in words to this effect:

"At no time while I am helping you with this or any other problem will your problem become my problem. The instant your problem becomes mine, you will no longer have a problem. I cannot help a person who hasn't got a problem.

When this meeting is over, the problem will leave this office exactly how it came in: on your back. You may ask for my help at any appointed time, and we will determine what the next move will be and which of us will make it.

In those rare instances where the next move turns out to be mine, you and I will determine it together. I will not make any move alone."

The leader follows this same line of thought with each staff member until, at about 11:00 a.m., she realizes that she no longer needs to shut her door. Her monkeys are gone! Those monkeys will return by appointment only, and her commitment to her appointment calendar will ensure this. The leader is helping her team accept their responsibilities and grow.

Remember, the key elements here are respect and confidence. You respect your staff's abilities and have confidence they can and will continue to grow and develop skills with your support. Think of it this way: you can keep tying a child's shoes every day. It doesn't take long each time you do it, but by not teaching the child to tie his shoes, you are saying he can't have cool sneakers. He isn't competent enough to have them. Have the respect and confidence in those you brought onto your team. Show them how to do the thing and to support them in developing the skills needed to succeed. Air Jordan's await!

For me, the best way to practice this skill was to use it as often as I could. That means that this has become a lifestyle. Honestly, I forgot it when my kids were in elementary and middle school. I spent a lot of time doing stuff for them and others who were just not my monkeys. Thankfully, I relearned my lesson and regained balance as they entered high school.

Transferring the Initiative

With this monkey-on-your-back analogy, we have been aiming to transfer initiative from superior to staff. We also aim to learn to keep it there. We have tried to highlight a truism as obvious as it is subtle. Namely, before developing initiative in staff, the leader must ensure that they have it.

Once the leader takes the initiative back, staff members no longer have it, and discretionary time can be kissed goodbye. It will all revert to staff-imposed time.

Both leader and staff cannot effectively have the same initiative at the same time. The opener, *"Boss, we've got a problem,"* implies this duality and represents a monkey astride two backs, which is a very bad way to start a monkey's career.

So, let us take a few moments to examine what we prefer to call "The Leadership Action Plan." There are five degrees of initiative that the leader can exercise in relation to the boss and to the system. These are listed in order from lowest to highest:

(1) wait until told

(2) ask what to do

(3) recommend, then take resulting action

(4) act but advise at once

(5) act on their own, then routinely report

Clearly, the leader should be professional enough to refrain from indulging in Initiatives 1 and 2 in relation either to the boss or to the system-imposed time.

A leader who waits until told has no control over either the timing or content of boss-imposed or system-imposed time. In this case, the leader immediately forfeits any right to complain about what she is told to do or when. The leader who asks what to do controls the timing but not the content. Initiatives 3, 4, and 5 leave the leader in control, with the greatest control being at level 5.

The leader's job—in relation to staff initiatives—is twofold: first, to outlaw the use of Initiatives 1 and 2. This insists upon giving staff no other choice but to learn and master "completing staff work." Second, to see that for each problem leaving the office, an agreed-upon level of initiative is assigned to it. Each meeting is finished with the next meeting scheduled. The leader notes the meeting on her appointment calendar and happily watches the monkey riding piggyback out of her office.

Care & Feeding of Monkeys

To help explain our comparison between the monkey-on-your-back and the usual ways of assigning tasks and staying in control, let's talk about the leader's schedule. There are six important rules that guide the "Care and Feeding of Monkeys." Breaking these rules can waste valuable time.

Rule 1: Monkeys should be fed or let go. Otherwise, they will starve to death, and the leader will waste valuable time on post-mortems or attempted resurrections.

Rule 2: The monkey population should be kept below the maximum number the leader has time to feed. The leader or staff will find time to work as many monkeys as they find time to feed, but no more. It should take at most 5-15 minutes to feed a properly prepared monkey.

Rule 3: Monkeys should be fed by appointment only. The leader should not hunt down starving monkeys and feed them on a catch-as-catch-can basis.

Rule 4: Monkeys should be fed face-to-face or by telephone, never by email. Email changes the situation and makes the next move the leader's responsibility – remember? Documentation may be added to the feeding process, but it cannot replace feeding.

Rule 5: Every monkey should have an assigned next feeding time by appointment and a "degree of initiative." These may be revised at any time by mutual consent, although never allowed to become vague or indefinite. Otherwise, the monkey will starve or wind up on the leader's back. Always schedule the next feeding time before you leave a meeting.

Rule 6: Don't Chase the Monkey. When the leader chooses to chase a monkey, they search down and complete staff tasks when that monkey was not even given to the leader to feed. Time spent taking over someone else's responsibility disguises itself as discretionary time when the leader tries to help. Have you offered to do something for a family member, friend, or staff member because it was on the way, or were you already going to be there? You chased and took over that monkey.

Leaders running after monkeys demonstrates loss of control. Allowing the monkeys dictate the pace and priorities leads to a chaotic environment in which the leader's time and energy are spent on reactive tasks rather than proactive management.

Following the Care and Feeding of Monkeys rules ensures that the monkeys remain manageable and the leader stays in control. Allowing monkeys to dictate the terms disrupts the leader's schedule, undermines their authority and efficiency. The leader can learn to maintain a clear, structured approach to managing monkeys. This affords the leader more time and a more peaceful working environment. When monkeys are addressed promptly, and efficiently, unnecessary chasing is eliminated.

The first rule of monkey management is often the hardest one for people to get a handle on. It can be daunting to think monkeys should be fed or let go. Here is an example of let go of a monkey:

> Joanne: *Can I have next Tuesday off?*
>
> Leader: *Do you need an answer right now?*
>
> Joanne: *Yes.*
>
> Leader: *Then the answer is no.*

It *is that* easy. I use this phrase all the time to execute monkeys. Try it the next time someone interrupts you with a monkey. This is a great place to start. Believe me, your friends or family give you many opportunities to practice.

If they can't give you the time to consider the ramifications of their request, then you have to say no. To say anything else would be disrespectful.

Another way to let go a monkey is to ask if the person followed your procedure:

> Janice: *Can I have next Thursday off?*
>
> Leader: *Did you complete the 'day-off request' two weeks before the date?*
>
> Janice: *No.*
>
> Leader: *Then I cannot approve the day off. You can find someone to cover your shift. If you do, submit a completed 'shift coverage' form in the inbox.*

See? Not your monkey. It belongs to Janice. Creating systems for fending off monkeys like these is key to running a business without losing your mind. You need systems to create a monkey force field around you. Your standard operating procedures and employee handbooks are examples of tools to create your force field.

If you have decided to feed a monkey, that doesn't mean it has to stay your responsibility. You might simply be fostering the monkey until you can pass it off to a different caretaker, delegating the responsibility. Use delegation and take responsibility for your decisions and actions. Be aware that there is always a next move, and that's where knowledge will allow you to be better prepared.

In summary, anyone in any position can make life much easier by following a few simple rules and learning to manage monkeys well.

The first order of business is for the leader to enlarge her discretionary time by eliminating staff-imposed time.

The second is for the leader to use a portion of this newly created discretionary time to ensure that each staff member possesses the authority to exercise initiative. Then, the leader only has to see to it that initiative is taken.

The third is for the leader to use another portion of the increased discretionary time to get and keep control of the timing and content of both boss-imposed and system-imposed time.

The result of all this is that the leader's leverage will increase. This enables the value of each hour spent managing management time to multiply without theoretical limits.

Watch out for monkeys. The woods are full of them!

Chapter 5

Helping You Spot and Deal with Monkeys in the Wild

Monkey Troupe Management

Remember that monkeys tend to multiply when left unattended.

You must follow the six monkey rules to keep your business functioning well!

#1 Feed or let go of the monkeys when you first see them.

#2 Keep the population to a manageable number.

#3 Monkeys are to be fed by appointment only.

#4 Feeding occurs face to face, not by text or email.

#5 Monkeys should be assigned the next feeding time and degree of initiative.

#6 Never chase a monkey.

As you practice troupe management skills, we want to help you name the different monkeys who will work hard for you to adopt them. Each of these monkeys have a common call that you will hear loud and clear as well as easy predetermined defenses you can employ to ward them off.

Idea Monkey

This monkey most frequently appears at staff meetings or gatherings. Feeds off goodwill and enthusiasm and can be easily defended against.

Common calls: This monkey can be identified with calls such as, "I have a great idea for a carnival," and "have you thought about reworking all the office layouts?"

Defense: The defenses include "great idea, here is the planning form," "what will be the funding source for this," or "I like where this is going, get a group together and keep us updated."

Payday Monkey

This monkey tends to lurk in doorways. It is most often sighted three days before paychecks are being issued. Its favorite foods are pity and flexibility. Its primary attacks are sad stories and tears.

Common calls: You can identify it by its distinctive cries of, "Can I have a cash advance," "I need more hours because" and, "I will be late with paying for the product or service you provided."

Defense: If it attacks, giving it time off from your business is an excellent diversionary tactic.

Wuss Monkey

Often found in the office behind a closed door or in a room with only one other adult. It is a sensitive primate and usually avoids interacting with more aggressive monkeys. It hides and throws out passive-aggressive barbs when no one is looking. It feeds off of concerns over program morale.

Common calls: It has distinctive calls such as "I have a problem with this person. Can you handle it for me? " and " How do you think this person's issues should be handled?"

Defense: This monkey is best handled by open, honest, and private conversations between the Wuss Monkey and its targets.

Problem Monkey

Roams freely and is rarely found in engaged classrooms.

Common calls: This monkey can be identified with calls such as "How should I handle this issue?" and "Can you please come? A person is doing a thing I don't understand/like."

Defense: It can be handled by holding it accountable. Examples include "What are three ways to address this?" and "How was this handled when you were young?" Additionally, matching the monkey with a know-it-all monkey can be successful.

The Chatty Monkey

The Chatty Monkey wants a minute of your time, but that minute can easily become 30 or 45. They have lots to share with you.

Common calls: This monkey can be identified by calls such as " Have you heard about this?" and "Do you have a minute?"

Defense: The primary management technique for this breed is planned time with them. Meeting regularly to chat keeps them from attacking you unawares and upsetting the flow of your workday

Know It All Monkey

The Know-It-All Monkey surfaces frequently around slow periods or cleaning times. It preys upon idle hands and can be handled by delegating to them.

Common calls: This monkey can be heard with calls such as "The next room doesn't have their new project up yet" and "Have you read this article about language development techniques?"

Defense: This type of monkey needs projects to keep it out of mischief. Try pairing it with newer staff, giving them projects, etc.

To Do Monkey

The To Do Monkey does not linger but can be seen briefly in texts, notes left on your desk, or phone calls. The food source must be precisely determined, but it can be fended off.

Common calls: Calls can include, "Could you get this for me at the store," "Could you call this client back," or "Could you give this message to my coworkers," although their calls can be particularly varied.

Defense: Post-it notes can be an excellent way of corralling this pesky little monkey, as is a published schedule. Create a schedule as part of your standard operating procedures. Having clear times when phone calls are made, supplies ordered, and rooms visited conditions this monkey into a rhythm in which their needs are met before they become an issue.

The Tattle Monkey

The Tattle monkey is like the know-it-all monkey, although it does have different behaviors and seems to feed primarily on perceived injustice or shirking of duties.

Common calls: "Sandra clocked in 15 minutes before she started working," "It's not fair that..." or "Did you know that so and so was doing this and that?"

Defense: The best defense against their attacks is a focus on professionalism and confidentiality.

The Assistance Monkey

The Assistance Monkey is often mistaken for an assistant but lacks follow-through, causing it to drain time, energy, and patience from the person being assisted. This monkey appears lazy and untrustworthy as they shirk responsibilities.

Common calls: "I can do that" and "I have a great resource for that."

Defense: It doesn't need to be defended against; simply trained. Utilizing the steps to proper delegation, this monkey can become an asset. If left unattended, however, the building will become littered with half-completed projects and disappointed people.

Manage My Time Monkey

The Manage My Time Monkey can be found in the workspaces you walk through or on notes left on your desk. It is especially aggressive when you have deadlines or are about to leave the building. It feeds off perceived free time, and attacks can include "but you are so good at that kind of thing".

Common calls: Its calls are among the most varied in the primate family. Prime examples include, "Can you watch my station? I need to run to the bathroom," and "Can I have next Wednesday off?"

Defense: The best defensive strategies include, "That sounds like a great plan. I will check in with you on Monday to see what progress you have made," and "You know where the form is located for that request, right?"

Whatever you do, *Don't Chase the Monkey!*

Chapter 6

Rule 1: Monkeys Should Be Fed or let go

In the world of management, "monkeys" represent tasks, responsibilities, or issues that land on your desk. These monkeys demand attention, but how you handle them will determine your effectiveness as a leader. The first rule is simple: Monkeys should either be fed or let go. If you neglect them, they'll starve, leading to wasted time on post-mortems or attempts to bring them back to life. But how do you make sure you're handling these monkeys properly? Let's explore 10 ways to "let go" monkeys which eliminates your tasks. Let's also discuss 10 ways to "feed" monkeys, managing tasks, without causing chaos.

10 Ways to let go Monkeys

1. Delegate Effectively

   Identify tasks that can be handled by someone else on your team. Clearly define the task, set expectations, and let them take leadership. Delegating frees you from the burden of handling every task personally.

2. Say No

   Only some tasks or requests deserve your attention. Learn to say no when a task doesn't align with your priorities or when it's something that others can handle. Protect your time for what truly matters.

3. Automate Routine Tasks

   Use technology to automate repetitive tasks. Whether it's scheduling, reporting, or data entry, automation tools can take these monkeys off your plate permanently.

4. Set Clear Boundaries

   Establish boundaries with your team and peers. If a task is not your responsibility, communicate that clearly. Encourage others to handle their monkeys rather than push them onto your desk. It is important to note that a boundary is not a request. A boundary is your active response to your boundary being compromised.

5. Simplify Processes

   Analyze and streamline workflows to eliminate unnecessary steps. By simplifying processes, you reduce the number of tasks that require your intervention, effectively let going multiple monkeys at once.

6. Delegate Decision-Making

   Empower your team to make decisions within their areas of responsibility. This reduces the number of decisions you need to make, freeing you from the burden of micromanagement. It also reinforces your confidence in them and develops teammates self-esteem.

   "But what if they make the wrong decision?" I hear you

asking. You have made plenty of wrong decisions in your life, and to this point, none of them have been fatal, right? They will make the occasional bad decision, which you will work together to rectify. Most people will make many more good decisions than bad decisions. If you are unwilling to allow failure, you are unwilling to innovate and adapt.

Let them fail occasionally. It is good for the culture.

7. Outsource Non-Core Tasks

   Consider outsourcing tasks that are outside your core competencies. Whether it's administrative work, IT support, or specialized services, outsourcing allows you to focus on what you do best. Do what you are best at doing and hire out the rest.

8. Eliminate Unnecessary Meetings

   Meetings significantly drain time. Eliminate unnecessary meetings and replace them with concise communication methods like email updates or shared project management tools.

9. Use Time-Blocking

   Block out specific times in your schedule for focused work. During these times, turn off notifications, ignore all distractions and focus solely on high-priority tasks. This approach helps you let go down minor monkeys that could otherwise consume your day.

10. Decline Leadership of New Monkeys

    When introducing a new task or responsibility, evaluate whether it truly belongs to you. If not, decline leadership and choose who should handle it. This prevents new monkeys from multiplying on your desk.

Bonus: This response from chapter 4 is a true gem: Do you need an answer right now?

10 Ways to Feed Monkeys Without Creating a Feeding Frenzy

1. Prioritize Tasks

   Feed the most important monkeys first. Prioritizing your to-do list ensures you pay attention to the critical tasks and handle the less important tasks later. Why spend time right this minute planning next year's holiday party when you need to pay this month's bills and write the order list of supplies?

2. Ask Questions

   When someone brings up an issue, ask them questions. "What have you tried?" "What are 3 possible other ways to address this issue?" "Who might have some experience with this type of issue?" "What are your next steps?"

3. Break Tasks into Manageable Pieces

   Large tasks can feel overwhelming, leading to procrastination. Break them down into smaller, manageable pieces, and feed the monkey one bite at a time.

4. Set Clear Deadlines

   Assign clear deadlines for each task. This keeps the monkey alive and ensures regular feeding, preventing a crisis later.

5. Schedule Regular Check-Ins

   Schedule regular check-ins with your team or with yourself to monitor progress on tasks. This keeps the monkeys fed without letting them multiply uncontrollably.

6. Focus on One Task at a Time

   Multitasking leads to inefficiency and mistakes. Focus on feeding one monkey at a time to ensure that each task is handled properly before moving on to the next.

7. Communicate Expectations Clearly

   When delegating tasks, clearly communicate what needs to be done, how it should be done, and when it's due. This ensures that the monkey is fed correctly and doesn't come back to haunt you.

8. Use Task Management Tools

   Utilize task management tools like Trello, Asana, or Microsoft Planner to organize and track your tasks. Use a corkboard and index cards if tech solutions are outside your comfort zone. You've got this! These tools help you keep your monkeys in line without creating chaos.

9. Limit the Number of Tasks You Take On

   Be realistic about how many tasks you can handle at once. Limit the number of monkeys on your desk to a manageable level to avoid a feeding frenzy.

10. Delegate with Guidance

    When delegating, offer guidance and support without micromanaging. This ensures the task is done right the first time, keeping the monkey healthy without overwhelming your team.

Bonus: Regularly reflect on how you're managing your tasks. If you notice certain monkeys growing too large or out of control, adjust your approach to feeding them more effectively.

How you handle your to-do items—your "monkeys"—will determine your effectiveness and sanity as a leader. The key is to either feed or let go each monkey before it has a chance to grow or multiply out of control. By let going unnecessary tasks and feeding the important ones properly, you'll maintain a balanced workload and prevent chaos from taking over.

The strategies above offer practical ways to manage your tasks without letting them overwhelm you. Whether you're delegating, automating, or prioritizing, each method designs a system to keep your monkeys in check. As you continue your management journey, remember that the goal is not just to survive the day-to-day demands but to thrive as a leader who can handle anything that comes your way.

This is just the beginning. Mastering the art of managing your monkeys is a lifelong process. The more you practice, the better you'll identify which monkeys need to be fed, which need to be let go, and how to do so without creating chaos. Your adventure as a leader is full of choices—make sure you're choosing wisely and keeping your monkeys in line.

Chapter 7

Rule 2: Keep the Population to a Manageable Number

AKA: Monkey Containment Devices

In the jungle of management, where to-do items or your "monkeys" constantly vie for attention, it's crucial to contain them properly. Monkeys can run wild without effective containment, multiplying and overwhelming your ability to manage them. To prevent chaos, every leader needs reliable "monkey containment devices"—tools like notebooks, planners, and clipboards that help you keep track of your tasks.

The fundamental principle of Rule 2 is simple: The monkey population should be kept below the maximum number you and your team can feed. This means that you need to be realistic about how many tasks you can effectively manage in a day and use your containment devices to ensure that you don't take on more than you can handle.

The Importance of Containment

Containment isn't just about organization—it's about survival in the world of management. Wild monkeys scatter, create confusion, stress, and lead to ultimate failure. Containment devices are your first line of defense. Containment devices assist you to:

1. Prioritize Tasks: Identify which monkeys need attention first.

2. Track Progress: Ensure that each monkey is fed regularly and doesn't starve.

3. Maintain Focus: Prevent distractions by keeping your tasks visible and manageable.

4. Limit Overload: Keep your monkey population in check, ensuring you're not overwhelmed by too many tasks at once.

The effectiveness of your containment depends on the tools you choose. Each device has its strengths, and the right combination will depend on your personal preferences and work style. Here's how you can use notebooks, planners, and clipboards to keep your monkeys under control.

Notebooks are classic tools for capturing ideas, to-do lists, meeting notes, and more. They are versatile and portable, making them ideal for leaders who are constantly on the move. You can use a notebook to quickly jot down tasks as they arise, ensuring that nothing slips through the cracks. By dedicating a page each day to your most important tasks, you maintain a clear focus on what matters most. At the end of the day, reviewing your notes and transferring any unfinished tasks to the next day's page helps keep you organized. Using different sections of your notebook for various types of tasks, such as urgent versus long-term, can help you prioritize and manage your workload effectively.

Planners are specifically designed to organize your time, making them essential for tracking deadlines, appointments, and long-term goals. You ensure that no responsibility is neglected by allocating specific time slots in your planner for each task. Planners are also excellent for setting weekly or monthly goals and breaking down larger projects into manageable steps. Listing tasks in order of priority ensures that the most critical ones are addressed first. The key to effective planning is consistency, so choose a planner that suits your style—whether daily, weekly, or monthly—and stick with it.

Clipboards may seem old-fashioned, but they are incredibly effective for keeping active tasks front and center. They are handy for tasks that require mobility or need to be shared with a team. Attaching your most urgent or time-sensitive tasks to a clipboard keeps them visible and ensures they are remembered. You can also create checklists on your clipboard for recurring tasks or project steps, checking off items as you complete them to get a clear view of progress. For team management, clipboards can track delegated tasks, allowing you to monitor who is responsible for each task.

Setting up the Containment for Success

Once you have chosen your tools you will effectively manage your tasks. It's crucial to ensure that the number of tasks you take on never exceeds your capacity to handle them.

Start by assessing your capacity—understand your limits and use your tools to track and assess your workload regularly. If you notice that tasks are piling up faster than you can complete them, it may be time to delegate or eliminate some tasks. Set time limits for each task, ideally taking no more than 5-15 minutes to complete. If a task takes longer, break it down into smaller, more manageable parts to prevent burnout and keep your tasks moving forward.

Review your tools regularly at the end of each day or week. Identify tasks that have not been completed and consider whether they need to be delegated, simplified, or eliminated. Regular reviews help you stay on top of your workload and ensure no task is left unfinished.

Avoid overloading yourself by resisting the temptation to take on more tasks than you can handle. If your notebook, planner, or clipboard is full, it's a sign that you need to prioritize your current tasks before adding new ones.

Feeding the Monkeys Efficiently

Efficient feeding means allocating the right amount of time and attention to each task. Here are some strategies to ensure your monkeys are well-fed without creating a feeding frenzy:

- Batch Similar Tasks: Group similar tasks together and tackle them in one go. This reduces the mental load of switching between different types of tasks.
- Use Alarms and Timers: Set a timer for each task. This helps you stay focused and ensures you don't spend too much time on any one monkey.
- Delegate Wisely: Don't feed every monkey yourself. Delegate tasks that others can tackle, freeing up your time for more critical responsibilities.
- Avoid Perfectionism: Not every monkey needs a gourmet meal. Feed them adequately. Don't waste time trying to make every task perfect.

In the jungle of management, effective containment is the difference between order and chaos. By using notebooks, planners, and clipboards, you can keep your monkeys in check, ensuring that you never take on more than you can handle. Remember, the goal is not just to survive but to thrive as a leader. By managing your monkey population wisely, you'll maintain control over your workload, reduce stress, and achieve greater success in your role.

Your journey as a leader is all about making the right choices—starting with how you contain and manage your monkeys. Choose your tools wisely, stay within your limits, and you'll find that even the wildest jungle can become a well-tamed garden.

Chapter 8

Rule 3: Monkeys Should Be Fed by Appointment Only

In the fast-paced business management environment, it's easy to fall into the trap of addressing tasks and responsibilities as they come—reactively tackling whatever issue screams the loudest at any given moment. But this "catch-as-catch-can" approach leads to inefficiency, stress, and missed opportunities. Rule 3 is clear: Monkeys, those tasks and responsibilities, should be fed by appointment only. Establish a structured schedule for managing tasks rather than allowing them to disrupt your day randomly.

It's easy to feel overwhelmed by the sheer volume of tasks, responsibilities, and decisions that bombard you every day. From managing staff and maintaining compliance with regulations to ensuring the safety and well-being of those in your care, the weight of your role can often feel like too much to bear. What if I told you that this feeling of overwhelm is not only common but also conquerable?

Building initiative-taking systems for scheduling when you will accept, or feed monkeys is a key element of your defense strategy.

The Importance of Scheduled Feedings

To understand the importance of scheduled feedings, let's revisit a day in the life of our leader. In the first version of the day, she arrives at work already feeling the weight of a growing to-do list. Before settling in, she's bombarded by a supervisor needing urgent feedback on a project, a staff member whose car broke down, a child who needs her attention, and a flood of emails demanding immediate responses. Each of these monkeys represents a demand on her time and energy. Without a system in place to manage them, she finds herself constantly reacting, never able to get ahead or focus on the tasks that truly matter.

In the second version of the day, the leader implements the third rule of monkey management. She knows that monkeys will always be there. Instead of letting monkeys dictate her day, she sets specific times to address them. She communicates to her leader that she will review the leader's project at a set time, sets a time for Tommy to call in if he needs help solving his transportation issue, and checks email before heading out to collect monkeys during the walkthrough. By only feeding monkeys by appointment, she can maintain control of her schedule, reduce stress, and focus on high-priority tasks.

This shift from reactive to proactive management allows the leader to be more effective in her role and sets a clear expectation for her team. They learn that while their needs are addressed, they must wait until the appointed time. This encourages them to be more independent and less reliant on immediate responses.

Feeding your monkeys by appointment is not just about organization—it's about control. Without a schedule, tasks can quickly spiral into disorder, leading to burnout and a chaotic work environment. Scheduling time to handle specific tasks fosters:

1. Improves Focus: Concentrate on one task at a time, ensuring it receives your full attention.

2. Increases Efficiency: Complete tasks more quickly and

effectively when they're given dedicated time slots.

3. Reduces Stress: Eliminate the constant pressure of unfinished tasks looming over your head.

4. Enhances Predictability: Know exactly what needs to be done and when, making planning your day easier.

5. Maintain Work-Life Balance: Avoid the endless work cycle by setting clear boundaries for when tasks will be addressed.

Establishing a Feeding Schedule

Creating a feeding schedule for your monkeys involves more than just setting aside time. It requires a thoughtful approach to prioritization, time management, and discipline. This process develops a strategic approach to handling your work, ensuring that each task gets the attention it needs without overwhelming your day.

The first step is to assess your daily and weekly responsibilities thoroughly. Begin by listing all the tasks that demand your attention. This list should be comprehensive, capturing everything from quick, routine tasks like checking emails to more substantial commitments such as project management or strategic planning.

Once you have this list, categorize these tasks based on their urgency, importance and required time. Understanding the scope of your responsibilities in this way allows you to allocate your time more effectively. Daily tasks—those that must be completed every day—should be clearly identified, while tasks that can be managed weekly should be noted separately.

Next, it's important to prioritize your tasks, recognizing that not all monkeys are created equal. Some tasks will require immediate attention due to their impact on your business or looming deadlines, while others can afford to be scheduled later.

Prioritizing becomes key. Tackle high-priority tasks first, ideally at the beginning of your day when your energy and focus are at their peak. Conversely, schedule lower-priority simpler tasks when you need a break from more demanding work. By applying a prioritization framework, such as the Eisenhower Matrix, you can more effectively determine the order to address tasks.

After prioritizing your tasks, allocate specific time blocks for each task. This approach, often called time blocking, prevents tasks from bleeding into each other and focuses your attention on completing each task before moving on to the next. A good habit to adopt is dedicating the first hour of your day to planning.

Following planning with a set time for team check-ins or a walk-through sets a good pace for your team as well. Include buffer time between tasks to accommodate unexpected issues and to give yourself a breather. Realistic time allotments for each task are crucial here. Overloading your schedule is a recipe for stress and inefficiency.

An effective feeding schedule benefits from regular review meetings. These meetings, whether conducted with your team or simply as a self-assessment, show you where you get off track and should make necessary adjustments. A weekly review can provide an opportunity to assess your progress and plan for the upcoming week. A daily check-in helps confirm your priorities and adapt to any changes in your schedule. These reviews help clear up any confusion, reassess priorities, and ensure all tasks progress as planned.

The success of feeding your monkeys by appointment hinges on discipline and consistency. Treat each scheduled task as a meeting with yourself. When you meet with a client or colleague, you respect the time set aside for them, right? You deserve the same respect. Resisting the urge to deviate unless necessary. During your allocated task times, eliminate distractions—turn off notifications, close irrelevant tabs, and focus solely on the task at hand.

If a task cannot be completed within the designated time, don't let it spill over into the next block. Instead, reschedule the remainder of the task for another dedicated time. Take note in the future that this task may need smaller bites of shorter tasks or more time allotted for completion. Your commitment and consistency ultimately keep your monkeys well-fed and under control. This allows you to manage your responsibilities with greater ease and effectiveness.

Dealing with Emergencies

Even with a well-planned schedule, emergencies will arise. When they do, you want a plan to address them without derailing your entire day.

Develop the skill of distinguishing between a true emergency and a monkey that can wait. Emergencies are situations in which immediate action is necessary to prevent significant harm or disruption. When these arise, it's appropriate to pause your scheduled feeding and address the issue.

However, many so-called "emergencies" are simply monkeys that feel urgent but aren't truly critical. By maintaining a feeding schedule, you'll become better at recognizing the difference. Training your team to handle non-emergencies independently or wait until the scheduled time alleviates the urgent calling cries of demanding monkeys.

- Emergency Time Blocks: Consider setting aside some time each day as a "flex" or "emergency" period. This allows you to handle unexpected tasks without disrupting your entire schedule.
- Assess and Reschedule: If an emergency requires you to shift your schedule, assess which tasks to postpone or delegate. Reschedule these tasks promptly to ensure they're not forgotten.

Scheduling Tip: Be careful to use emergency time sparingly. If emergencies become a regular occurrence, it may be a sign that your schedule needs reevaluation, tasks need better planning or your staff requires.

The Benefits of Scheduled Feeding

Feeding your monkeys by appointment creates a structured, predictable environment where tasks are managed efficiently and effectively. This approach enhances productivity, reduces stress, and improves the quality of your work. Having more predictability in your day reduces the feeling of being overwhelmed by constantly reacting to demands. This control also increases productivity, so you can focus on important tasks without constant interruptions.

Scheduled monkey management fosters a culture of independence and problem-solving within your team. When they know that their issues will be addressed at a specific time, they are more likely to try solving problems on their own or find ways to manage until the scheduled time. This empowers your team and frees you up to focus on the big picture.

Finally, scheduled feeding helps you maintain a healthier work-life balance. By managing your time more effectively at work, you're less likely to bring unfinished tasks and stress home with you, leading to better overall well-being.

Feeding your monkeys by appointment only keeps your tasks under control but is so much more! It's about mastering the art of time management. By establishing a structured schedule, prioritizing effectively, and maintaining discipline, you can ensure that your to-do items are handled efficiently without the stress of constant monkey wrangling. .

As you implement this rule, you'll find that your work becomes more focused, your days more productive, and your monkeys far less troublesome. Remember, the key to success as a leader isn't just in completing tasks, it's about effectively managing your time. Feed your monkeys by appointment and watch as they snuggle peacefully, and you see your productivity—and your peace of mind—soar.

Chapter 9

Rule 4: Monkeys Should Be Fed Face-to-Face

In the world of management, communication is key. Your communication directly impacts how effectively you can manage your tasks—your "monkeys." Rule 4 emphasizes that monkeys should be fed face-to-face or, if that's not possible, by telephone or video call—never by email or text. This rule is grounded in the understanding that certain tasks require direct, personal interaction to be managed effectively.

While convenient, emails and texts often create more problems than they solve when it comes to managing tasks. It can lead to misunderstandings, delays, and a lack of accountability. Ultimately this "quick" communication leads to making the task management process more cumbersome.

The Risks of Email Feeding

Feeding your monkeys through electronic communication can be tempting. After all, it's quick, easy, and doesn't require a direct conversation. However, this convenience often comes at a cost.

One of the primary risks is lack of clarity. Emails lack the nuances of tone, body language, and immediate feedback, which are critical in ensuring that messages are interpreted correctly. According to a study by Professor Albert Mehrabian, only 7% of communication is based on the actual words used, while 38% comes from tone of voice and 55% from body language. Without these nonverbal cues, the message can easily be misinterpreted, leading to confusion and mistakes. This is particularly problematic in situations where the stakes are high, or the task is complex. I don't know about you, but the idea that only 7% of what I'm trying to get across is being received is not acceptable. So, I step up and have actual conversations.

Delayed responses make electronic communication subpar. Emails can sit in inboxes, waiting for the recipient to respond. Delays slow down progress, causing tasks to stall and monkeys to starve. In a fast-paced environment, such delays can be detrimental, leading to missed deadlines and increased frustration. We all know someone (Carrie raises her hand) who doesn't respond to emails as often as others may expect.

Additionally, emails often result in a shift in responsibility. When you send an email, you might think you've successfully passed the monkey on to someone else. However, the responsibility often bounces right back to you. When the recipient doesn't respond promptly or requires further clarification this can create a never-ending loop of back-and-forth communication. This back-and-forth becomes both time-consuming and inefficient.

Another significant risk associated with email communication is no accountability. Without direct, personal interaction, it's easier for people to ignore or procrastinate on tasks. There's no immediate accountability, which can lead to tasks being neglected or completed half-heartedly.

Increased miscommunication is another common pitfall of email. The lack of personal touch necessary for complex or sensitive tasks can lead to damaged relationships, missed opportunities, and tasks being done wrong. Miscommunication via email can result in frustration, resentment, and even conflict, further complicating task management.

Given these risks, the best approach to feeding your monkeys is to do so face-to-face whenever possible. This allows for the full spectrum of communication—words, tone, body language—to be used effectively, ensuring the message is clear and understood. If face-to-face interaction isn't feasible, the next best option is a video call. Video calls capture most of the nonverbal communication cues, including facial expressions and tone of voice, which are crucial for conveying the full meaning of your message.

If video isn't an option, a telephone call should be your last resort. While it lacks the visual component of communication, it still conveys tone, rhythm, and intonation, which are critical for ensuring that your message is understood as intended. Textual communication, on the other hand, strips away these vital elements, leaving too much room for misinterpretation.

You Can't Text a Banana: The Importance of Face-to-Face or Phone Communication

Feeding your monkeys through direct communication—whether face-to-face or by phone—is essential for ensuring that tasks are clearly communicated, fully understood, and promptly addressed. Unlike emails or texts, which can easily be misinterpreted or ignored, direct communication allows for an interactive exchange where both parties can engage dynamically. This not only ensures that the task is properly conveyed but also confirms that it has been received and understood.

One of the key advantages of direct communication is the ability to gauge the other person's response in real time. You can spot signs of reticence, confusion, or discomfort, which might not be apparent in written communication. If you notice these signals, it's a cue to pause, restate your points, or ask for feedback. This interactive process ensures that both parties are on the same page and that any misunderstandings are addressed immediately.

Reflective listening is a crucial component of this process. By actively listening and reflecting on what you've heard, you can confirm that the other person has indeed grasped the task at hand. For instance, after explaining a task, you might ask, "So, what steps will you take to get the project done?" This reinforces clarity and gives the other person a chance to voice any concerns or ask for further clarification.

Additionally, the emotional nuances that come with tone, rhythm, and intonation are crucial for conveying the importance and urgency of a task. Studies have shown that up to 92% of communication is non-verbal, meaning it's conveyed through facial expressions, body language, and tone of voice rather than words alone. This underscores why face-to-face interactions, or at least phone calls, are so vital. They allow you to convey the full context of your message, ensuring that the other person truly understands the task and its significance.

This type of communication fosters accountability. When someone looks you in the eye or hears your voice directly, they are more likely to feel a personal responsibility for completing the task. This is far less likely to happen through email, where the impersonal nature can lead to a sense of detachment from the task.

Bad Outcomes When You Don't Feed Face-to-Face

The consequences can be severe when you rely on email instead of direct communication. Here are some examples of what can go wrong:

1. Miscommunication: A simple request sent via email can be misunderstood, leading to a task being done incorrectly or not at all. For example, a vague email asking a team member to "handle the client issue" could result in the wrong action being taken, damaging client relations.

2. Task Neglect: Without immediate direct communication, tasks can be easily forgotten or deprioritized. An email might get lost in the inbox or go to another folder, leading to delays and missed deadlines.

3. Escalation of Issues: If a sensitive issue is communicated via email, it can escalate due to the lack of personal touch. A team member might misinterpret the tone and feel undervalued or attacked, leading to conflict and decreased morale.

4. Loss of Trust: Relying too heavily on email can erode trust within your team. Team members might feel that you're not invested in their work or that you're avoiding difficult conversations, leading to disengagement.

Using Your Best Self for Effective Feedings

To manage your monkeys effectively through direct communication, you must leverage your strengths—your "best self." Empathy is a key quality to bring to these interactions. By using your ability to understand and share the feelings of others, you can connect more deeply with your team during task discussions. This connection fosters better communication and stronger relationships.

When you detect these signs, it's important to engage in reflective listening. Restate the key points of the task and ask for the other person's feedback. This gives them the opportunity to confirm their understanding or express any concerns they might have. By doing so, you create a dialogue that ensures the task is fully understood and that the other person is committed to completing it.

Remember, the goal is not just to hand off tasks but to ensure that they are received, understood, and acted upon effectively. This level of engagement is what makes direct communication so powerful—it allows for a true exchange of ideas and ensures that tasks are managed with the attention and care they deserve.

Active listening is another crucial skill. It involves focusing on truly hearing what the other person is saying—not just listening to respond but listening to understand. This approach lets you grasp the full scope of the task and any concerns the other person might have, ensuring that the task is well understood, and that the person feels supported.

Confidence is also important. When you confidently approach each conversation, you can communicate the task at hand clearly and assert the importance of its timely completion. Confidence helps convey that the task is a priority and that you believe in the person's ability to accomplish it.

Clarity is essential in these interactions. Being clear and concise ensures that the task is understood without room for misinterpretation. If necessary, reiterate key points to make sure everything is crystal clear.

Finally, patience is vital, especially when explaining complex or new tasks. Taking the time to ensure that the person fully understands the task and feels supported can make all the difference in whether the task is completed successfully.

By utilizing these qualities—empathy, active listening, confidence, clarity, and patience—you can enhance your direct communication and ensure that your monkeys are fed effectively, keeping your projects on track and your team motivated.

Best Practices for Face-to-Face and Phone Communication

To truly master the art of direct communication, particularly in the management of your tasks—or "monkeys"—it's essential to follow a few best practices. These guidelines ensure that your communication is not only clear but also effective in driving the desired outcomes.

1. Prepare in Advance: Before discussing a task, make sure you're clear on what needs to be done. This will help you communicate the task more effectively.

2. Set Clear Expectations: Be specific about what you expect from the task, including deadlines, desired outcomes, and any necessary resources.

3. Follow-up: After the initial conversation, check in to ensure the task is on track. This reinforces accountability and shows that you're invested in the task's success.

4. Be Available: Make sure your team knows they can reach out to you if they need clarification or assistance. Being accessible fosters open communication and trust.

5. Document When Necessary: While direct communication is key, documentation can still play a role. After a face-to-face or phone conversation, consider sending a brief follow-up email summarizing the key points discussed. This provides a reference and helps prevent any misunderstandings.

Let 's see how this might look. Imagine you're leading a team that's been tasked with launching a new product. You have a critical conversation with your marketing leader, Erica, about developing the campaign strategy. Before the meeting, you take the time to outline the key goals and milestones you expect from the campaign. During your face-to-face discussion, you clearly communicate these expectations, set specific deadlines and highlight the resources available to her team. Erica listens attentively, but you notice a slight hesitation when you mention the timeline.

Instead of brushing past it, you pause and ask for her feedback. Erica expresses concern that the timeline might be too tight, given the current workload. You take the time to engage in reflective listening, acknowledge her concerns and ask her to suggest a more realistic timeline. Together, you agree on a revised schedule that still meets your overall goals. After the meeting, you send a quick email summarizing the revised plan, ensuring that both of you are aligned.

In this scenario, your preparation allowed you to communicate effectively, your awareness of Erica's hesitation enabled you to address potential issues early, and your follow-up email ensured that there was a clear record of your conversation. By embracing these best practices, you not only managed the monkey effectively but also strengthened your working relationship with Erica. You set the stage for a successful campaign launch.

Mastering the art of direct monkey feeding is about more than just talking; it's about engaging in meaningful, dynamic conversations that drive results. By preparing thoroughly, setting clear expectations, following up, being available, and documenting, when necessary, you ensure that your monkeys are well-fed, and your management skills are continually refined. Remember, effective communication is the cornerstone of successful management—embrace it, and watch your team thrive.

Mastering the Art of Direct Monkey Feeding

In the world of management, effective communication is the cornerstone of success. By feeding your monkeys face-to-face or by telephone, you ensure that tasks are handled efficiently, relationships are strengthened, and your team remains engaged and accountable.

Remember, you can't text a banana—and you can't rely on email to effectively manage your tasks. Embrace direct communication, leverage your best self, and watch as your monkeys are well-fed, and your management skills reach new heights.

Chapter 10

Rule 5: Always Schedule the Next Feeding Time

Before you leave a monkey meeting, you must schedule the next feeding. Every monkey should have an assigned next feeding time by appointment and a "degree of initiative." These may be revised at any time by mutual agreement, but they should never be allowed to become vague or indefinite. If they do, the monkey is at risk of starving or, worse, ending up back on your shoulders.

This is called delegation. You might have heard of it before. You may have even tried it, only to see it fail. But remember, just as you didn't learn to walk on your first attempt, mastering delegation takes practice and persistence. When you assign a monkey to someone else, you're delegating responsibility. You must follow up to ensure that the monkey stays off your back.

Imagine a team member approaches you and asks you to change their work schedule. You have decided to feed the monkey, saying you're fine with the idea, provided they can find someone to cover their shifts. If you leave it here, that monkey is going to starve to death, and you will have a mad employee who thinks you won't let them change shifts. I know you said yes, if they found coverage, but there was no follow-through. He will likely forget that it was his monkey to manage. Instead, add rule 5. "Come back Friday at 4:00 after you have discussed the schedule with the other team members." Now the monkey is fed and has a next feeding time, all tied up in a bow of his level of initiative.

As a leader, Carrie left her business for two to three weeks every year. I would often work three-day weeks and enjoy long weekends with kids and spouse. I'm not a mind-reader, but you are probably asking yourself, *"How in the world is that glorious possibility even remotely possible?"*

The answer lies in a combination of strategic business closure and effective delegation. Carrie would close her business for a period, allowing her and her staff to enjoy the same vacation time. She paid her staff during this time off, which boosted retention and saved money in the long run. By doing this, she avoided the headache of scheduling individual vacations and scrambling for temporary help.

The second part of Carrie's strategy was delegation. She made sure her team knew who was in charge and divided responsibilities while she was away. Initially, she checked in twice a day to ensure everything was running smoothly. But as her confidence in her team grew, she reduced these check-ins to once a day, knowing they would contact her in an emergency. She had clearly defined what constituted an emergency—something like a no-show for a shift did not make the cut, but a 911 call did. By delegating effectively and providing her team with a high level of authority, Carrie could enjoy her time off without worry.

Achieving this level of freedom didn't happen overnight. In the early years of her business, Carrie focused on building the systems needed to secure time away. Her motivation was clear—she wanted the flexibility to do what she wanted, when she wanted. She had a favorite vacation spot that took two days to reach by car. If she only took one week off, travel time would eat up four days, leaving her with just four days to enjoy. To make longer vacations possible, Carrie created systems that allowed her to leave her business in capable hands, confident that her team could handle any situation that arose.

I became a master at scheduling and packing in work during the day. Informing my clients what work would be finished before and after the time on vacation alleviated interruptions and managed expectations.

Then we just enjoyed the time away, leaving town or even the state. Bear in mind that this did not happen during our first year as new business leaders. We had not created the systems needed yet to secure time away from managing the business.

Proactively, I made a goal to do this as soon as I could. Remember how goals need motivation? Well, I had it! Carrie did. too. She and I wanted to have the flexibility to do what I wanted when I wanted.

To reach this point, Carrie and I needed a solid delegation plan. We developed our own methods for delegating and planning, understanding that effective delegation is a process that can vary from person to person.

The delegation process itself is straightforward but requires careful consideration. Start by asking yourself seven key questions:

1. What are the elements of the task?
2. What are the abilities of the person to whom I want to delegate the task?
3. What resources are available to complete the task?
4. What outcomes are expected?
5. When is the task due?
6. When are progress reports due?
7. When will you be available to consult on the task?

With these answers in hand, you can assign the task to someone well-suited for it and provide the necessary support. The bigger challenge often lies in deciding what tasks to delegate. When I last tried to list all the monthly activities a leader handles, I recorded over 120 items. That's a lot to accomplish in a 40-hour workweek, which is why many leaders end up working more hours and eventually burning out.

You cannot do it all. You just can't.

As they say in the song, *"Love is like a magic penny. Hold it tight and you won't have any. Lend it, spend it, give it away."* The same is true for work. You already have so much it could be rolling all over the floor! Lend it out to others. It helps them and you.

Start by outsourcing some tasks. This might involve eliminating unnecessary activities, automating tasks you dislike, or delegating your staff. Many tasks you think are essential are often just fluff. For example, you can connect your accounting software to the bank and set up auto-responders. Delegating tasks, like an employee creating this week's supply order, can significantly reduce your workload.

When deciding what to delegate, consider which tasks you excel at and what you enjoy. If you're good at something and it brings you joy, don't delegate it—that's part of what makes your work fulfilling. But if you're not good at something and you dislike doing it, find another way to get it done. Automate it, delegate it, or as the saying goes, "hire it done."

I challenge you to make a list of everything you know you'll be expected to do as a leader. Write it all down. Then, see what can be automated—start there. Delegate to a computer by setting up automated billing notices. If you've already done that, consider creating and automating a series of welcome emails for new clients. Create it once, and then let a computer carry it forward.

Think about what you do repeatedly for every client. Find a way to do it for the last time, automatically.

Delegation is not just about handing off tasks; it's about creating systems that allow you to focus on what truly matters. By mastering delegation, you can free up your time, reduce your workload, and create a business that runs smoothly—even when you're not there.

Create a grid like this and place all the items needing to be done within it.

The *Skill/Will Matrix - Desire and* Ability *grid.*

To effectively delegate tasks, it's crucial to understand your team members' abilities and desires. A useful tool for this is a grid that categorizes tasks based on skill level and interest. Group your tasks into four categories:

- Tasks to delegate with some guidance
- Tasks you love to do yourself
- Tasks to delegate with specific directions
- Tasks to delegate that someone else will love more than you

First, identify the tasks you're highly skilled at but not particularly interested in. These go in the top left section of the grid. Below that, place the tasks you're neither interested in nor good at. The top right quadrant is reserved for the tasks you both enjoy and excel at—this is your Zone of Genius. The bottom right corner is for tasks you love but may not be very good at. For Carrie, anything creative fits into this category, while for Kate, it's anything that resembles a craft project.

Don't delegate tasks that fall into your Zone of Genius. This is where your passion and expertise come together, making these tasks both enjoyable and essential to your role. On the other hand, delegate as much as you can from the lower left corner—these tasks neither interest you nor play to your strengths.

If you're not yet comfortable with delegating, plenty of resources are available, from books to YouTube videos and podcasts. Spend time exploring these options but remember that not every method will work for everyone. The key is to find an approach that resonates with you.

Remember The 7 P's

To get things done, it helps to remember this sentence of seven P's:

Prior planning prevents personally pathetic poor performance.

This mantra emphasizes the importance of preparation in successful delegation. Proper planning will not only make your life easier but will also create a more positive work environment for your team.

Effective delegation can transform your business's culture and improve job satisfaction for everyone involved. When done right, it leads to more time for you, an atmosphere of trust and respect, utilizing your team's highest skills, and promoting professionalism.

Recap of How to Delegate:

1. Plan what needs to be delegated
2. Select the person
3. Meet with the person
4. Create a plan of action
5. Inform the other faculty members
6. Implement the plan
7. Follow up
8. Remember to thank the person!

Delegation is not just about getting tasks off your plate; it's about empowering your team, promoting growth, and maintaining your own boundaries. Proper delegation increases efficiency, empowers employees, encourages skill development, enhances decision-making, and prevents burnout.

Principles of Effective Delegation

Effective delegation involves clear communication, assigning both responsibility and authority and matching tasks to team members' skills. It also requires providing the necessary resources and support, setting clear deadlines and milestones. Most importantly, delegation requires trusting your team. Feedback and recognition are crucial to reinforce positive behavior and motivate your team.

When deciding which tasks to delegate, start by identifying tasks that others can manage. Routine, repetitive tasks are often prime candidates. Then, select the appropriate team member based on their skills, experience, and workload. Clearly define the task, expected outcomes, and any constraints, and make sure the team member understands the importance of the task within the broader organizational objectives.

Steps to Effective Delegation

Delegation is a multi-step process. It starts with identifying the tasks that can be delegated and selecting the right person to handle them. Once the task is assigned, it's essential to clearly define expectations, assign both responsibility and authority as well as monitor progress without micromanaging. Regular feedback and recognition upon task completion are also vital to the process.

Overcoming Delegation Challenges

Delegation isn't without its challenges. Fear of losing control, lack of confidence in team members, poor communication, inadequate follow-up, and delegating too much too soon are common issues that can hinder effective delegation. However, these challenges can be overcome by gradually increasing the level of responsibility you delegate, providing opportunities for learning and development, ensuring clear and concise communication, and establishing a system for regular check-ins and progress updates.

Mastering the art of delegation is essential for any leader. It maximizes productivity, fosters professional growth, and ensures efficient resource use. By following these principles and overcoming common challenges, you can build a more capable and engaged team, driving success for your organization and yourself.

Chapter 11

Our Rule 6: Don't Chase the Ding Dang Monkey

The sixth rule of monkey management is never chasing the monkey. This is the hardest rule for most people new to the monkey management concept. Heck, it's probably the hardest concept for most people, period.

As a boss, I was horrible at chasing monkeys. I wanted my staff to like me. I instigated an open-door policy. My staff would come in and chat. I had comfortable chairs, and the space was great. But it meant that they would come in and chat. As people sat down their monkeys would just drop off their backs and run around my office. At the end of the visit, people would gather up their monkeys and get ready to go, and I would tell them I wanted one or two of those cute little primates.

One time a team member told me about a project she was planning. I found myself outlining steps to complete the project and brainstorming people that would be helpful in my notebook. I did this while I counseled her for poor attendance and assigned a corrective action plan. Get this...really get this: she didn't ask for help. Even worse she was insulted when I showed her all my helpful ideas, steps, and resources.

She showed me her monkey. I chased after it, snuck it away from her when she wasn't looking, and then returned it to her, all dressed up in fancy clothes. The result? She was offended. This was a wake-up call! I needed an intervention.

Why do we chase the monkey? There are a good number of reasons. Most of them have to do with our personal psychology. We'll get to that later. Right now, let's talk about why it is a bad idea to chase monkeys.

Chasing the monkey demotivates our staff, distracts us from what we should be doing and devalues other people's efforts. You want to have an active and engaged team that has initiative and involvement in the work that they are doing. You want to have a sense of accomplishment at the end of the day that you have achieved something. Sometimes the thing you have achieved is managing someone else's monkey. Does that go along with your goals and values as a leader?

Why do we Do It?

OK, let's explore why we chase the monkey. The biggest reason that we chase the monkeys is that we're trying to be helpful. We want to ease others' burdens, share our experiences, and shorten the period that someone else is in pain or discomfort.

Sometimes we do it because we're afraid of being disliked or being seen as bitchy. You know that people like other people who do things for them. It is an easy route to friends and companionship. Who doesn't like someone who brings them a cup of coffee and a cookie? There is a fine line between being of service to others and being generous or chasing other people's monkeys.

If you are someone who saw phrases like, "shows excellent leadership potential" on their grade school report card, this has a lot to do with why you take other people's monkeys. Taking the lead is part of your identity. You don't like to be seen as bossy and disengaged. To show that you are engaged with your staff, you try to help them with their problems. I get it. That is very, very noble of you. Here's a question: If you're feeling good about yourself more important than the other person's self-esteem?

The third reason I want to talk about that I know I chase monkeys, is to demonstrate competence. I became a leader in my early 20s. It was very important to me to be seen as competent and knowledgeable. One of the ways I did that was by solving other people's problems. This became part of my management style. It took a lot of work for me to unlearn this pattern of behavior. I took it so far as to be codependent in many of my relationships. I knew I could do the work, so I did, whether the other people could or should be doing that work.

The last reason I'm going to discuss, although surely not the last reason there is, is control. If you do everything that needs to be done inside of your business, it will be done to your standards. You have control. There is something very comfortable in knowing that everything is done just the way you like it.

However, if you are going to do everything in your business exactly the way you want it done, why are you bothering to have employees? You hired these people to be part of your team. They bring different abilities, skills and perspectives to your business. Those are valuable. That means that sometimes things are going to be done in a way different than you would do it yourself. Ceding control is one of the hardest things to do. I see you and I know that you can, you've got this!

Acting is much more comfortable than watching others try to do what you could do when they fail. You know how to plan the event. You have planned so many events over the course of your life that you couldn't count that high. But you and I both know that planning the event is not the best use of your time as the leader. So, you're going to have to be uncomfortable and live with the discomfort of delegating and letting other people handle their responsibilities.

When they fail, and they will, you help them pick themselves up, dust themselves off and get back into the groove. And when they succeed, and they will, you celebrate with them. It will be a great party!

Consequences of Chasing Monkeys

I can't tell you exactly what will happen in your business if you chase monkeys. But I can give you some examples of what happened in mine and Carri's lives when we chased monkeys. Perhaps you can learn from our mistakes.

Story 1: A staff member asked to speak to me privately saying they were very distracted and just needed me to give them a little bit of patience and grace today. I asked what was going on. Their answer was not something I ever thought I would be dealing with in a work environment. They thought their sister was in an abusive relationship. They had no idea what to do. Worrying about their sister having kept them up all night long was going to be a distraction during the workday. I'll let her vent all the while knowing I could help with this problem. When she felt ready to go to work, I gave her a hug and we moved on with our respective days, her to her job and me chasing her monkey.

I spent several hours looking up all of the resources for battered women in our area. I reached out to colleagues for counseling resources for this unknown sister. I found companies that would move her for free. I found various living arrangements that the sister could use with either free or discounted rent. There was nothing that I could think of that I had not found a resource for this woman, this woman I had never met. My heart ached for both my employee and her sister. I knew I could make it better.

At the end of the day, I called my employee over and gave her all the resources I had collected. None of those resources included how to talk to someone in an abusive relationship who has not yet realized that their relationship is abusive. My employee was thankful for the help and then let me know that their sister did not live in the area.

What came out of that day? I spent half of my day doing work that was not helpful. I let my employee know that I saw and heard her concerns and that I was there to support her.

And... I gave her a bunch of paper that she would never be able to use. I could have accomplished the one positive outcome from this situation without spending half of my day and creating a whole bunch of recyclable paper. If I had just asked her what help she needed, my time would have been better used and she would have gotten more effective support.

Story 2: For coffee with a friend, I listened to her while she complained that her spouse had not actually planned anything for their vacation. She was very sad that they had this time off from work and had nothing to do because her partner hadn't held up his obligations. I commiserated and said that that stunk. As soon as we were done with the coffee, I whipped out my handy dandy computer and went to work finding alternatives and fun things they could do in a staycation. I found free things, inexpensive things and elaborate things as I did not know their budget. I functioned as my friends free travel agent. Once I was done, I emailed it over to my friend, secure in the knowledge that I had been an excellent friend.

Here's the thing, me chasing that monkey robbed her and her spouse of the opportunity to work through the consequences of his lack of action. I stole away the lesson she could learn about following the steps of effective delegation. This could have been an opportunity for them to work on communication and deepen their commitment to each other. Instead, I contributed to resentment building up in their relationship. By doing the work for them I allowed them to avoid consequences and lessons to learn from their failures.

Story 3: One of my children said he wanted a new job. So, of course, I chased that monkey. I went online and found 20 different jobs that he could apply for. When he didn't apply for all the jobs that I had found for him, I got frustrated and grumpy with him. Couldn't he see that I was trying to help him? He expressed a desire for a new job, and out of the goodness of my heart, found him a bunch of good options for new jobs. I knew how to find places to apply. I had done it dozens of times in my life, so I knew what to do. By me doing it for him instead of showing him how to do it, I robbed him of a learning opportunity. I also took away the natural effects of accomplishment. I did not allow him to feel the pride and confidence of doing it himself.

None of these stories worked out the way I thought they would. As a reformed monkey-chaser, I could go on and on. I have a list of five more stories right here in front of me, but that might be me chasing the monkey for you! I want to give you an idea, a snapshot of what it looks like when you chase the monkey. At this point you probably have a bit of an idea of how this generally turns out. I'm going to go ahead and write down the beginnings of the next few stories and you can use your imagination to see where it may go.

- Your parents have health conditions they don't want to admit they have.
- You paint a room that someone complained about.
- You potty train your grandchild without being asked.
- You are a prereader for a book, and you decide to completely edit it.
- Your mother's business partner dies, leaving your retired parent working 80-hour weeks in a high stress job, so you decide to help.

Designing an Environment that Discourages Monkey Chasing

I learned that creating an office arrangement that minimizes staff hanging around promotes productivity, collaboration, and efficiency involves thoughtful design and strategic placement. I recommend two firm chairs and a table outside of your workspace. For most of us that means two wooden chairs and a side table on the other side of the desk from you. Comfy chairs, sofas, ottomans, and other soft elements encourage people to spend a lot of time in your office.

That means you aren't getting your work done and neither are they.

You can proactively eliminate many monkeys chasing by starting with your office. Create an office environment that minimizes the risk of monkey chasing. That starts with intentional design and organization. Your workspace should be set up in a way that promotes focus, productivity, and efficiency while subtly discouraging staff from offloading their responsibilities onto you. One of the most effective ways to achieve this is by carefully considering the layout of your office. For instance, placing your desk in a position where you're not directly facing the door can reduce the likelihood of someone dropping by unannounced and staying longer than necessary.

Additionally, opting for functional, firm seating rather than plush, inviting chairs can help limit the time staff spends in your office. When your space feels less like a lounge and more like a place of work, it subtly communicates that conversations should be purposeful and efficient.

Maintaining an open-door policy is essential for fostering communication and collaboration, however, it needs to be balanced with the need to avoid unnecessary distractions. One strategy is to establish "office hours"—specific times during the day when your door is open for drop-ins and quick discussions.

Outside of these hours, encourage staff to schedule appointments for non-urgent matters. This approach allows you to be accessible without sacrificing your productivity. It also helps your team understand that while you're available to support them, your time is valuable and needs to be managed effectively. You might also consider using a visual cue, like a sign on your door or desk, indicating whether you're available for impromptu meetings or need to focus on deep work.

Clear boundaries are crucial for preventing monkey chasing, and these boundaries must be communicated and reinforced consistently. It's important to set expectations with your team about what types of issues warrant immediate attention and which can wait until a scheduled meeting. For example, you can establish a protocol for urgent matters that genuinely require your intervention versus those that can be handled independently or with minimal guidance.

Once these boundaries are in place, it's vital to uphold them consistently. If a team member tries to offload a monkey onto you outside of the agreed-upon processes, gently, but firmly redirect them, reminding them of the protocol. Over time, this consistent reinforcement will create a culture where everyone respects each other's time and responsibilities, leading to a more efficient and harmonious work environment.

Chasing Real Monkeys

As we talked about writing this book and more, we shared our theories with others - I wanted to share the viewpoint of chasing monkeys from a literal sense.

Chasing monkeys is an activity fraught with ethical, practical, and ecological concerns, making it inadvisable for several compelling reasons. Understanding the implications of such behavior is essential for promoting responsible wildlife interaction, preserving ecological balance, and ensuring human safety. Here are the primary reasons why one should refrain from chasing monkeys.

First, chasing monkeys is ethically questionable. Monkeys, like all wildlife, deserve to be treated with respect and consideration. They are sentient beings capable of experiencing stress, fear, and pain. When humans chase them, it causes unnecessary stress and can lead to injury or psychological trauma. This behavior is a form of harassment that disrupts their natural behavior and can lead to long-term adverse effects on their well-being. Respecting wildlife means observing from a distance and not interfering with their natural activities, ensuring that we do not cause them harm or distress.

Chasing monkeys poses significant practical risks to humans. Monkeys, particularly in regions where they are accustomed to human presence, can become defensive or aggressive if they feel threatened. This can result in bites or scratches, which not only cause physical injury but also carry the risk of transmitting diseases such as rabies or simian herpes B virus. These infections can be serious and sometimes fatal to humans. Furthermore, in an attempt to escape, monkeys might enter hazardous areas such as roads or other dangerous environments, increasing the risk of accidents that could harm both the animals and humans.

From an ecological perspective, chasing monkeys can disrupt local ecosystems. Monkeys play a vital role in their habitats, contributing to processes such as seed dispersal and maintaining the balance of their ecosystems. Disturbing their natural behavior can have cascading effects on the environment. For instance, stressed or displaced monkeys might avoid certain areas, leading to overgrowth of some plants and underutilization of others. Altering the vegetation dynamics impacts the environment and other species dependent on those plants. Ensuring that monkeys can perform their ecological roles without human interference is crucial for maintaining biodiversity and ecological health.

Educationally, observing monkeys' behavior in their natural surroundings offers far more value than chasing them. Learning about their social structures, communication, feeding habits, and interactions with their environment can provide insights into primate behavior and broader ecological principles. Encouraging respectful observation helps foster a deeper appreciation for wildlife and promotes conservation efforts. By observing monkeys calmly and quietly, individuals can gain a better understanding of these fascinating creatures and contribute to the broader goals of wildlife conservation.

There are legal and conservation implications to consider. In many regions, wildlife protection laws prohibit harassing or disturbing animals. Violating these laws results in fines or other legal consequences. Additionally, unethical behavior towards wildlife undermines efforts aimed at protecting endangered species and preserving natural habitats. By chasing monkeys, individuals inadvertently contribute to the negative perception of tourists and locals, which hinders conservation initiatives and the implementation of protective measures.

Chasing monkeys is inadvisable due to ethical concerns, practical risks, ecological impacts, educational considerations, and legal implications. Observing them without interference respects wildlife. We secure their well-being, preserve ecological balance, and promote a culture of respect and conservation. By understanding and adhering to these principles, we enjoy and learn from our interactions with wildlife while contributing to their protection and the health of our natural world.

Respect and Boundaries in Professional and Personal Relationships

In both professional and personal relationships, the impulse to help others by taking on their responsibilities can often stem from good intentions. However, this behavior—as we call it "chasing the monkey"—can inadvertently convey a lack of respect for the other person's abilities and autonomy. In the workplace, this dynamic can lead to resentment and inefficiency, while in personal relationships, it can create dependency and imbalance.

One of the most iconic examples of this dynamic in popular culture is the relationship between Michael Scott and Dwight Schrute in The Office. Michael, as the regional leader, often takes on tasks that should be Dwight's responsibility, either out of a desire to be liked or a misguided attempt to help. Dwight, eager to please and prove himself, sometimes pushes tasks onto Michael without intending to, knowing that Michael will take over. This results in chaos. Michael overextends himself and Dwight never fully develops the independence needed to excel in his role. While Michael may think he's helping, he's stunting Dwight's professional growth and creating a cycle of dependency.

In personal relationships, this dynamic can be equally problematic. Consider the relationship between Lorelai and Rory Gilmore in Gilmore Girls. Lorelai often steps in to solve Rory's problems, sometimes without being asked. While her actions are motivated by love and a desire to protect her daughter, they sometimes prevent Rory from navigating challenges independently. This dynamic creates a scenario where Rory may rely on her mother's intervention rather than developing the skills needed to handle issues independently, leading to tension as Rory matures and seeks her own path.

Respecting and creating healthy boundaries allows others to manage their responsibilities. It's important to recognize that overstepping—whether by taking over a task, solving a problem uninvited, or micromanaging—diminishes the other person's sense of leadership and achievement. In a professional context, this not only impacts the individual's confidence but leads to a culture of dependency in which employees are reluctant to take initiative or make decisions. This dynamic can be observed in the relationship between Don Draper and Peggy Olson in Mad Men. Draper, a brilliant domineering figure, often makes decisions for Peggy, who is eager to prove herself. While Draper's mentorship is invaluable, his tendency to overshadow her efforts can stifle Peggy's creativity and drive, making it harder for her to assert her voice.

The consequences of chasing someone else's monkey can be even more profound in family dynamics. For instance, when a parent constantly steps in to solve their child's problems—be it in school, friendships, or early career challenges—they risk creating a dynamic in which the child never learns to stand on their own two feet. This over-involvement leads to dependency, lack of resilience and leaves the child ill-prepared to face life independently.

In friendships, the act of chasing someone else's monkey blurs the lines between support and overreach. Friends are meant to be there for each other, offering help and advice when needed. However, taking over a friend's responsibilities or trying to solve their problems for them leads to resentment. It suggests that you don't trust your friend to handle their own life, which erodes trust and equality in the relationship. For example, in Friends, Monica's overbearing tendencies often lead her to try and control the lives of those around her. She has organized Chandler's job search and even dictated Rachel's love life. While her intentions are good, her actions sometimes strain her relationships as her friends push back against her well-meaning yet intrusive behavior.

Respecting others' abilities and maintaining healthy boundaries means recognizing when to step back and allows people to manage their own tasks and challenges. It is about offering support without taking over, providing guidance without dictating actions, and trusting that others will effectively manage their responsibilities.

This approach fosters personal and professional growth and strengthens relationships by building mutual respect and trust.

In the workplace, this means trusting your team members to complete their tasks and encouraging them to take leadership of their work. Delegating involves setting clear expectations, providing the necessary resources, and then stepping back to let them execute. When leaders chase the monkeys of their team members, they inadvertently communicate that they do not trust their team to perform. In personal relationships, to avoid the chase means to recognize the importance of individual agency.

Supporting your loved ones while watching them face their own challenges and grow shows respect and trust. Whether it is a spouse, child, or friend, giving them space to navigate their own life is an act of respect and love. It acknowledges their capability and reinforces the idea that they do not need to be rescued or managed but rather supported and believed in.

Ultimately, not chasing the monkey fosters independence, respect, and healthy boundaries in all areas of life. Balance by learning when to help, when to step back, when to offer guidance and when to allow others to take the lead. By mastering this balance, you create an environment where everyone can thrive, free from the burden of unnecessary interference.

When you choose to complete these tasks even when the monkey was not specifically given to you to feed. Time spent taking over someone else's responsibility seems like discretionary time when the leader tries to help. Have you offered to do something for a family member, friend, or staff person because it was on the way, or you were already going to be there? This is taking or chasing a monkey.

Recognizing When You're Chasing a Monkey

In any professional or personal relationship, there comes a moment when you might find yourself on the brink of taking on a task that is not yours—stealing a monkey. Recognize these moments to maintain balance and respect in your interactions.

Identify the Signs

One of the first signs that you are about to chase a monkey hide within yourself. You feel a sudden shift in your thoughts and emotions when you feel an urge to "just help out" or "make things easier" for someone else. This might happen when a colleague mentions a challenging task. If you instantly start planning how to do their work, you could easily chase down and steal that monkey.

Learn to stop yourself at this red flag stage. Catch yourself before you catch another monkey. Another telltale sign is when you feel a rising sense of obligation, even though the task was never explicitly assigned to you. If you notice your thoughts spiraling into solution mode for a problem that is not yours, it's a red flag that you're about to grab someone else's monkey. At the first awareness of your red flag, train yourself to make a new choice to support rather than hunt down monkeys.

Consider how Michael Scott from *The Office* often jumps into situations, attempting to "fix" problems that are not his to solve. His catch-as-catch-can approach usually leads to more chaos.

Similarly, Ross from *Friends* frequently finds himself entangled in situations with Rachel or his sister Monica, when his well-intended interventions complicate matters. See how easy it is to chase a monkey without realizing it?

Pausing to Assess

Recognize your red flags. Before you leap into action, pause, and ask yourself a few key questions: Is this really my responsibility? Has this person asked for my help, or am I offering unsolicited advice? What are the potential consequences of my taking this on? This crucial pause allows you to assess when you are about to overstep your own boundaries.

Reflective listening plays a critical role here. By truly listening to the other person, you can determine if they are seeking advice, merely venting, or asking for help. Repeating what you have heard to ensure you've understood their needs correctly. For example, if a colleague says, "I'm struggling with this project," you might respond, "It sounds like this project challenges you. What support do you need to move forward?" This opens the door for them to clarify whether they need help or need to express their frustrations.

Practical Tools and Scripts

When you realize that the monkey is not yours to take, create practical tools or scripts to decline tasks politely. For example, say, "I'm confident you have the skills to manage this. If you need specific support, I'm here to help you find the right resources." This response acknowledges their abilities while setting a clear boundary. Another approach could be, "I'm currently focused on my own projects, but I'm happy to brainstorm ideas with you." This way, you offer support without taking on their responsibility.

Create a supportive environment in which team members feel empowered to manage their own responsibilities. This encourages autonomy and provides the tools needed to succeed. Do so without stepping in to do the work for them. In *Friends*, consider how

Chandler supports Joey in pursuing his acting career—offering advice and encouragement but allowing Joey to navigate his own path. This dynamic respects Joey's autonomy while reinforcing their trust.

Create a Supportive Environment

In a well-functioning team or relationship, everyone will feel empowered to manage their own responsibilities. Leaders and peers will build trust and foster a culture in which asking for help is encouraged but avoids overstepping. Providing the right resources, training, and support without taking away the individual's leadership of their tasks marks a strong leader.

In the workplace, this involves scheduling regular check-ins with team members to discuss their challenges and seek advice without feeling pressured to offload their responsibilities (Rule #3). In personal relationships, be a sounding board rather than a fixer.

Allow your loved ones to navigate their own challenges, without butting in and chasing down their monkeys. They will appreciate knowing you support them.

Recognizing when you are about to chase a monkey, pausing to assess, and using the right tools to maintain boundaries, you ensure that you are respecting both your own responsibilities and those of others. This helps prevent burnout and strengthens the trust and autonomy within your team and relationships. Your self-control leads to more effective and harmonious interactions.

Strategies to Avoid the Monkey Chase

Knowing how to avoid stealing someone else's monkey maintains a healthy balance of responsibilities. Here's how to say no politely, help without taking over, and ensure you're providing support without stepping into the monkey caretaker role.

Say "No" Politely and Assertively

It is easy to feel guilty declining to take on someone else's task.

Remember, saying no is acceptable and necessary. When someone tries to pass their monkey to you, a polite and assertive "no" can be your best defense. Consider phrases like, "I appreciate your trust in me, but I believe you're more than capable of handling this," or "I'm currently focused on my priorities, but I'm happy to discuss how you can tackle this." These responses are both respectful and clear, reinforcing your boundaries while showing confidence in the other person's abilities.

Help Others Without Taking Over

There is a fine line between being supportive and taking over someone else's responsibilities. To avoid crossing that line, offer guidance or resources rather than direct action. For example, if a colleague is struggling with a project, you might suggest tools, share your experience, or brainstorm potential solutions together.

However, resist the urge to step in and do the work yourself. This not only helps them grow but also keeps the monkey where it belongs—on their back, not yours.

Think Ross from *Friends* again. He helps Rachel navigate her career struggles. He offers advice and emotional support, but he refrains from making decisions for her. This approach allows Rachel to take leadership of her choices while Ross remains a supportive friend.

The Role of Follow-Up

Follow-up maintains support that does not turn into control. After offering advice or resources, ask about progress, but choose to avoid micromanaging. For instance, after a meeting in which you have discussed a challenge, a simple "How's it going with that project we talked about?" shows you care without implying that you will take over. Follow-up conveys accountability and encouragement, not reclaiming responsibility for the task.

Stay involved enough to provide support. You empower others' confidence to complete their tasks and reassure them of your continual support.

Mastering the Art of Letting Go

Learn to resist the urge to chase monkeys in both your professional and personal life. Letting others keep their monkeys respects their autonomy and prevents you from becoming overwhelmed by tasks that are not yours.

Embracing a balanced approach to helping others means offering support without taking over, guiding without controlling, and trusting in their abilities by maintaining your own boundaries. Be a leader or a friend who empowers others rather than someone who inadvertently disempowers them by taking on too much.

The long-term benefits of resisting the monkey chase are profound. You will find yourself with more time and energy to focus on your own priorities. You will create less stress, and stronger, more respectful relationships. Others will appreciate the trust and confidence you place in them, leading to a more collaborative and effective environment.

In the end, mastering the art of letting go is recognizing that you cannot—and shouldn't—do it all. By allowing others to manage their own responsibilities, you foster a culture of accountability, respect, and shared success. So, the next time you see a monkey headed your way, remember you don't have to chase it. Let it stay where it belongs and watch as your leadership and relationships flourish.

Chapter 12

The Calm After the Storm: A Life of Managed Time and Tamed Monkeys

Every business journey encounters challenges, triumphs, and countless moments of doubt. For the female entrepreneur, these challenges often multiply. The balancing act between professional ambitions, personal life, and the unique pressures of societal expectations feels like a constant battle with unruly monkeys. As the story moves into the next phase profound realization surfaces: it is possible to manage these monkeys, reclaim your time, and create a productive, deeply fulfilling life. Let us rewind to the beginning of our journey, where the chaos was at its peak.

Business and demands grew. Every day felt like a race against the clock, with no finish line in sight. Monkeys—those annoying distractions and endless tasks—pulled attention in a hundred different directions everywhere. Back then, the only way to survive seemed to depend upon working harder, sleeping less, and sacrificing more. The to-do list was never-ending, and personal time ...a distant memory.

For many leaders, this phase is all too familiar. The weight of responsibility, the fear of failure, and the relentless pursuit of success feels overwhelming. There comes a moment when something shifts—a moment of clarity when you realize that the life you are living is not sustainable. It is not about giving up; it is about finding a better way.

The turning point in your story comes with the decision to take control. The decision to manage time with intention and tame rampant running monkeys. It will start with minor changes. You will recognize monkeys as they arrive, decide to feed, or let go of them, set boundaries, say no to unnecessary commitments, and create a structured routine that honors both work and personal life.

These changes will not be easy. You must confront long-held beliefs about success and rethink the notion that busyness equals productivity.

One of the most transformative tools is the to-do list. These are your self-assigned monkeys. They should be the priority to complete the work only you can do. Your day will no longer be a chaotic jumble of tasks; it will become a strategic map for the day.

Prioritization, delegation, and time-blocking turn the list into a powerful ally rather than a source of stress. The monkeys did not disappear—they never do—they are managed. The monkeys are no longer in control. You learned to recognize which monkeys were most important and prioritize them. You learned how to delegate monkeys to your team. You learned how to set up routines to keep the monkeys from running wild. You created a jungle that works well in harmony. With time under control, a new world opens. The business thrives, not because of challenging work, but because of smart work. There is time to think, to strategize, and to grow—not just the business, but also personally. This is not just about making more money or expanding the business; it is about you living a fuller life.

For the female leader, this shift is particularly empowering. Breaking free from the traditional narrative, "success requires sacrificing personal happiness" equates to freedom. You show up for family, friends, and, most importantly, for yourself. Embrace the idea that self-care and downtime are not indulgences but necessities.

As business stabilizes and the monkeys are tamed, life begins to change profoundly. The constant stress and exhaustion will be replaced with a sense of calm and control. There is time for creative pursuits, deepening relationships, and self-reflection. The dream of having it all—a successful business and a fulfilling personal life—no longer seems impossible. It is a reality.

This better life has challenges, but it is balanced. The lessons learned along the way—about time management, boundaries, and self-worth—become the foundation for sustained success. The female business leader who once felt overwhelmed by monkeys running wild is now in control, confident, and content with monkeys contained in their new habitats.

The Ongoing Journey of Monkey Management

As this story reaches the next plateau, it is important to recognize that the journey of managing time and monkeys is ongoing. There will always be new challenges, distractions, and monkeys to tame. With the right tools and mindset, they will be managed. The life of a leader, with all its unique challenges, can be a life of joy, fulfillment, and success.

Even with effective strategies, new monkeys will always appear—and the key is to remain vigilant and adaptable. You will become comfortable with your new routine, and the people in your world will find new and inventive ways to try to offload their monkeys. If you start feeling like you do not have time for your priorities, STOP. Recognize the red flag. Take inventory, reread the relevant part of this book, and reinforce your routines and boundaries to keep the population of monkeys managed.

Personal Growth and the Art of Letting Go

This chapter is not just about managing time—it's about personal growth. As you master the art of letting go, you also learn to trust others to manage their own monkeys. This shift in mindset is a sign of maturity and confidence in your leadership abilities. It allows you to focus on what truly matters and to lead with clarity and purpose.

Creating a Supportive Environment: Fostering a culture in which everyone is responsible for their own monkeys, empowers your team to take leadership of their tasks. This not only frees up your time but also builds a more resilient and autonomous team.

The Long-Term Benefits: The long-term benefits of resisting the urge to chase monkeys are profound. You'll find that by letting go, you're not only reducing your stress but also giving others the opportunity to grow and succeed.

Embrace the Calm

The lessons learned here are universal, but they hold particular significance for women in business. They serve as a reminder that it is possible to create a life in which professional success and personal happiness coexist. The story of managing time and taming monkeys is a story of empowerment—a story of taking control of your life and shaping it into the life you have always wanted.

The journey is not over. There will always be new challenges and new monkeys. You now have the tools to manage them. Embrace the calm after the storm, and let it be a testament to your strength, resilience, and wisdom. The monkeys will always be there, do not let them run your life. You are the one in control, and that is the most powerful realization of all.

Chapter 13

Monday Morning Action Plan

Managing Monkeys in Volunteer Work, Family, and Children's Responsibilities

1. Prioritize Your Day with a Planning Session

- Action: Start your Monday by setting aside 15-20 minutes to plan your day. List out all the tasks, commitments, and responsibilities you have for the day, categorized under volunteer work, family, and children. If morning doesn't work well for you, the last thing in the evening the day before also works as well.
- Focus: Identify the most critical tasks that align with your long-term goals and personal values. These are your priorities.

2. Set Boundaries with Tasks and Responsibilities

- Action: Clearly define what tasks belong to you and what belongs to others. Write down specific roles and responsibilities for yourself and others in your different spheres (family, work, volunteer, social, etc.)

- Mantra: "I am responsible for my tasks, and others are responsible for theirs."
- Application: If someone shares their problems without directly asking for help, ask how you can support them without taking over the task.

3. Delegate Effectively

- Action: Assign tasks to others, regardless of the sphere, and trust them to complete their work in their own way. Avoid the urge to redo or micromanage unless essential for safety or compliance.
- Tip: Use clear communication to set expectations. Let go of the need for perfection in task completion. Sometimes good enough is good enough.

4. Time Block Your Priorities

- Action: Allocate specific blocks of time during your day for volunteer work, family responsibilities, and children's activities. Stick to these blocks as much as possible.

Example Saturday

- 9:00 AM - 11:00 AM for volunteer work,
- 11:30 AM - 1:00 PM for family errands, and
- 1:30 PM - 3:00 PM for children's activities or homework.

5. Implement the Don't Chase the Monkey Rule

- Action: When someone discusses their responsibilities or issues, do not automatically take on their tasks. Practice asking, "Are you asking for my help, or are you just sharing? "If they explicitly ask for your help, ask what help they might want before proceeding. Remember all the resources I accumulated for the abused woman who didn't even live in our area? Boundary: If they are sharing, listen and offer emotional support, but don't take on their burden.

6. Review and Adjust Your To-Do List Midday

- Action: Take a short midday break to review your progress. If necessary, adjust your to-do list, reprioritizing tasks based on what's been accomplished, the available time frame or what has shifted in importance.
- Goal: Ensure you stay on track and manage any newly arising "monkeys" without derailing your day.

7. Practice Self-Care and Reflection

- Action: At the end of the day, spend 10 minutes reflecting on what went well and determine what you will improve. Also, make sure to incorporate a moment of self-care, whether it's a walk, reading, or quiet time.
- Benefit: This will help you recharge and maintain a healthy balance between productivity and well-being.

8. Set Up for Tomorrow

- Action: Before ending your day, set up your workspace and create a preliminary plan for Tuesday. This helps you start the next day with clarity and purpose.
- Tip: Keep your focus on maintaining the boundaries you've set and reinforcing the delegation of tasks to others.

About the Authors

Kate Woodward Young, M.Ed. and Carrie Casey have been business partners since 1999 and cousins since 1971. As third-generation entrepreneurs raising the fourth generation, their business passions ignited in elementary school. Their interest in business began with parallel paths as Girl Scouts selling cookies. By their early twenties, they had engaged in MLM companies, party businesses, started nonprofits, franchises, and worked in their parents' enterprises.

Before turning twenty-one, they each launched their first business. Carrie established her first childcare center. Kate founded a printing business after her roles as a business analyst with the SBA and a WBE evaluator with WBENC. Over the next twenty-five years, they ventured into publishing companies, real estate developments, house flipping, and staffing agencies—experiencing all the highs and lows of entrepreneurship.

Their extensive journey has equipped them with invaluable insights, which they now share through speaking and writing as well as coaching and consulting. They have collectively mentored over five thousand entrepreneurs.

Other books by Kate and Carrie

Female Entrepreneurs

- Don't Chase the Monkey
- From Oh Sh*t to I Got This

Early Childhood Administrators

- More Than Tuition
- I Got This - Leadership Blueprint for Childcare Directors
- Don't Chase the Monkey
- 98 Things Your Childcare Teacher wants you to know-
- De estar Abrumado a "Entendido": La ruta de Éxito Garantizada para Dirigir un Centro de Atención Infantil (Guaranteed Success Route to Directing Your Childcare Center) (Spanish Edition)
- From Overwhelmed to I Got This

You can catch their podcast on all socials
@ChildcareConversations

www.ChildcareConversations.com

Made in the USA
Coppell, TX
18 January 2026